RESTful PHP Web Services

Learn the basic architectural concepts and steps through examples of consuming and creating RESTful web services in PHP

Samisa Abeysinghe

BIRMINGHAM - MUMBAI

D1300659

RESTful PHP Web Services

First published: October 2008

Production Reference: 1201008

Published by Packt Publishing Ltd.
32 Lincoln Road
Olton
Birmingham, B27 6PA, UK.

ISBN 978-1-847195-52-4

www.packtpub.com

Cover Image by Nilesh Mohite (nilpreet2000@yahoo.co.in)

Credits

Author

Samisa Abeysinghe

Reviewers

Md Emran Hasan

Suhreed Sarkar

Deepak Vohra

Senior Acquisition Editor

Douglas Paterson

Development Editor

Swapna V. Verlekar

Technical Editor

Siddharth .D. Mangarole

Editorial Team Leader

Mithil Kulkarni

Project Manager

Abhijeet Deobhakta

Project Coordinator

Rajashree Hamine

Indexer

Rekha Nair

Proofreader

Laura Booth

Production Coordinator

Aparna Bhagat

Cover Work

Aparna Bhagat

About the Author

Samisa Abeysinghe is Director, Engineering at WSO2. Samisa pioneered the Apache Axis2/C effort and architected the core of the Apache Axis2/C Web services engine. He continues to be an active contributor in the Apache Axis2/C project. His involvement in open-source projects began in 2004 when he started working with the Apache Axis C/C++ project.

Prior to his current role, Samisa played the project lead role for the WSO2 Web Services Framework for PHP project, which provides comprehensive support for building both SOAP and REST services and clients.

"No man is an island" — John Donne

As human beings, we do not thrive when isolated from others. This book was no exception. Many people contributed to the successful completion of this book, and I would like to acknowledge all those who contributed.

First, I must thank Douglas Paterson. Douglas, Senior Acquisition Editor of Packt Publishing Ltd., is the one who initially proposed to me that I write this book. And thanks to him, this book was born.

Next, my gratitude goes to Sanjiva Weerawarana, Founder, Chairman, and CEO ofWSO2, Inc. When I first consulted Sanjiva on his thoughts on whether I should be writing this book, he encouraged me and even offered to help.

Speaking about encouragement, I must thank my mother, who checked, on a weekly basis, if I was continuing with my work on the book and the progress that I was making on that front.

The staff at Packt Publishing Ltd. helped a great deal to make this book a reality. I would like thank Rajashree Hamine the project coordinator, Swapna Verlekar the development editor, and Siddharth Mangarole the technical editor. I would also like to thank all others from Packt Publishing Ltd. who contributed to this book in many ways.

I would also like to thank some of my WSO2 colleagues, who worked with me closely on the scripting projects, specially WSO2 WSF/PHP. I would like to mention Nandika, Dimuthu, Chinthana, and Buddhika. Though they did not work on this book directly, they helped me a lot to understand PHP while working on WSF/PHP.

About the Reviewers

Md. **Emran Hasan** is a web application developer, usability consultant, and a successful entrepreneur from Bangladesh. He has a Bachelor in Business Administration with MIS major and is currently pursuing his MBA. In his early days with programming, he developed a number of desktop-based business applications for clients all over the globe including US, UK, Canada, Australia, Malaysia, and Spain. Later he switched to the Web and started programming in PHP.

He developed the largest social community blogging platform in Bangladesh called "Badh Bhangar Awaj" (http://www.somewhereinblog.net), while working at Somewhere In Net Ltd. He then worked in Pageflakes (http://www.pageflakes. com)—two times "Web 2.0 Award" Winner for Start page and Trippert Labs, Inc. (http://www.trippertlabs.com)—which develops social software for large companies such as Electronic Arts.

Emran's work toolbox includes CodeIgniter and Zend Framework for rapid application development in PHP, MySQL, and SQLite for efficient data storage, jQuery & Dojo for feature rich UI, W3C valid XHTML and CSS for standard-compliant site layout, and strong Usability and Accessibility sense for pleasant user experience.

Currently Emran is leading his own web development company, Right Brain Solution Ltd. (http://www.rightbrainsolution.com), as the Chief Technical Officer. He is the technical lead and helps the company deliver industry-standard web solutions. When he is not working in his job or browsing around or replying to threads in the phpXperts group (http://tech.groups.yahoo.com/group/ phpexperts), he listens to music, reads book, and writes in his technical blog at http://www.phpfour.com.

Suhreed Sarkar is an IT consultant, trainer, and technical writer. He studied Marine engineering, served on board a ship for two years, and then started his journey in to the IT world with MCSE in Windows NT 4.0 track. Later he studied business administration and earned his MBA from the University of Dhaka. He has a bunch of BrainBench certifications on various topics including PHP4, Project Management, RDBMS Concepts, E-commerce, Web Server Administration, Internet Security, Training Development, Training Delivery and Evaluation, and Technical Writing.

As a trainer, he taught courses on system administration, web development, e-commerce, and MIS. He has consulted for several national and international organizations including the United Nations, and helped clients building and adopting their enterprise portals, large scale databases, and management information systems. He is a renowned technical author in Bengali—having a dozen of books published on subjects covering web development, LAMP, networking, and system administration. He authored *Zen Cart: E-commerce Application Development*, published by Packt Publishing.

While not busy with hacking some apps, blogging on his blog (www.suhreedsarkar. com), reading the philosophy of Bertrand Russel or the management thought of Peter F. Drucker, he likes to spend some special moments with his family. Suhreed lives in Dhaka, Bangladesh and can be reached at suhreedsarkar@gmail.com.

I would like to thank the team at Packt who provided excellent support to work on this book, especially Swapna Verleker and Rajashree Hamine. I am also grateful to my family and friends for allowing me to work on this.

Deepak Vohra is a consultant and a principal member of the NuBean.com software company. Deepak is a Sun Certified Java Programmer and Web Component Developer, and has worked in the fields of XML and Java programming and J2EE for over five years. Deepak is the co-author of the Apress book *Pro XML Development with Java Technology* and was the technical reviewer for the O'Reilly book *WebLogic: The Definitive Guide*. Deepak was also the technical reviewer for the Course Technology PTR book *Ruby Programming for the Absolute Beginner*, and the technical editor for the Manning Publications book *Prototype and Scriptaculous in Action*. Deepak is also the author of the Packt Publishing book *JDBC 4.0 and Oracle JDeveloper for J2EE Development*.

Table of Contents

Preface

This book discusses the use of PHP to implement web applications based on REST architectural principles. Web services are a popular breed of web application technologies in today's programmable Web, and REST is the most popular style used in there. This book uses real-world examples as well as step-by-step guidelines to explain how to design REST-style services and clients from the ground up and how to use PHP programming constructs and frameworks to implement those services and clients.

What This Book Covers

Chapter 1 introduces the concepts related to the programmable Web, shows how HTTP and web services are related to each other, introduces the principles behind REST, explains how HTTP verbs are used in REST applications, explains the need for RESTFul web services while building PHP web applications, and introduces some frameworks and tools that can be used to work with REST in PHP.

Chapter 2 takes a first look at REST with PHP. While providing and consuming REST-style web services, the primary pre-requisites are an HTTP server or an HTTP client library and an XML parser library. In this chapter, we will see how to use the PHP CURL API to consume web services using various HTTP verbs such as HTTP GET, POST, PUT, and DELETE. The DOM API and SimpleXML API for building XML object structures and parsing XML streams are also discussed. We will discuss in detail how to build XML request payloads and also how to parse XML response payloads. The final section of this chapter demonstrates how to use the HTTP client features and XML parser features to invoke the Flickr REST API.

Chapter 3 looks into some real-world applications and discusses how to combine multiple service interfaces to build value-added custom applications. In this chapter, we will see how to use RSS or ATOM feeds, Yahoo search API, and Yahoo maps API. With the know-how you gain in this chapter and the previous chapters, you could build very powerful value-added applications like mashups using publicly available REST-style services.

Chapter 4 covers the steps that you would have to follow in designing and implementing a resource-oriented service in detail. Identifying resources and business operations for a given problem statement, designing the URI patterns, selecting the correct HTTP verbs, mapping URI and HTTP verbs to business operations are covered using the library example. Implementing the services and business operations using PHP is explained in detail, step by step.

Chapter 5 covers the steps that you would have to follow in designing and implementing resource-oriented clients in detail. The design of the clients is governed by the design of the service. And the client programmer needs to understand the semantics of the service, which is usually communicated through service API documentation. In the examples of this chapter, we will use the library service API designed in Chapter 4 to explain how we could use an existing API while designing PHP applications.

Chapter 6 uses the REST classes provided with the Zend Framework to implement the sample library system. The design of the service and client are covered, along with the MVC concepts supported by the Zend Framework. We will discuss how resources map to the model in MVC, and how HTTP verbs when combined with resource URIs map to the controller in MVC. We will explore how to combine `Zend_Rest_Server` with `Zend_Controller` to implement the business operations of the service and how to use `Zend_Rest_Client` class to consume the services.

Chapter 7 looks into the use of tools to trace and look into the messages to figure out possible problems with request and response pairs passed between clients and services. That helps with debugging and troubleshooting of services and clients. We will also look into how we could look at the XML documents to figure out possible problems in building XML in this chapter, and discuss how we can locate problems in parsing incoming XML messages.

Appendix A introduces the WSO2 Web Services Framework for PHP (WSO2 WSF/PHP) and discusses how to use the WSF/PHP service API to implement the sample Library system as a REST service and implement a REST client to consume it. We will also look into using the SOAP features provided in the frameworks to implement a SOAP client to consume the same service using SOAP-style messages. This chapter also discusses the differences between REST and SOAP message styles, in brief.

Appendix B introduces a PHP class named RESTClient that can be used to consume REST-style services. This class supports all key HTTP verbs, GET, POST, PUT, and DELETE. The advantage of using such a class is that it minimizes the complexity of your client code. At the same time, you can re-use this class for all your REST-style client implementations. This PHP class is sufficient for most simple REST-style client programs, and requires no third-party libraries. However, if you want to implement services and also want advanced clients, it is advised to use a more established framework such as Zend Framework or WSO2 WSF/PHP introduced in Chapter 6 and Appendix A of this book.

What You Need for This Book

You need PHP5 installed with Apache httpd server to try out the samples of this book. You would require a MySQL installation to try out the library sample discussed in the book.

You also need to install Zend Framework and WSO2 WSF/PHP to try out the samples based on those frameworks.

Who This Book is For

This book is for PHP programmers who are interested in using Web Services in their applications. Sometimes, you would be interested in using the publicly available REST-style services in your own applications, in which case, the REST client concepts discussed in this book would be very useful. You might also be involved with the implementation of PHP applications where you want to expose some aspects of the application as services to the outside world, in which case, you can benefit from the REST service concepts covered in this book. In addition, if you are a software developer looking for a hands-on text that will help you understand REST principles, from the ground up, this book would be a very good guide for you.

Conventions

In this book, you will find a number of styles of text that distinguish between different kinds of information. Here are some examples of these styles, and an explanation of their meaning.

Code words in text are shown as follows: ISBN0001

A block of code will be set as follows:

```
<books>
    <book>
        <id>1</id>
        <name>Book1</name>
        <author>Auth1</author>
        <isbn>ISBN0001</isbn>
    </book>
</books>
```

New terms and **important words** are introduced in a bold-type font. Words that you see on the screen, in menus or dialog boxes for example, appear in our text like this: "clicking the **Next** button moves you to the next screen".

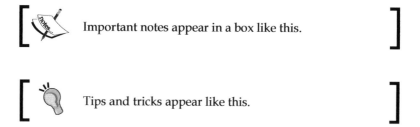

Important notes appear in a box like this.

Tips and tricks appear like this.

Reader Feedback

Feedback from our readers is always welcome. Let us know what you think about this book, what you liked or may have disliked. Reader feedback is important for us to develop titles that you really get the most out of.

To send us general feedback, simply drop an email to feedback@packtpub.com, making sure to mention the book title in the subject of your message.

If there is a book that you need and would like to see us publish, please send us a note in the **SUGGEST A TITLE** form on www.packtpub.com or email suggest@packtpub.com.

If there is a topic that you have expertise in and you are interested in either writing or contributing to a book, see our author guide on www.packtpub.com/authors.

Customer Support

Now that you are the proud owner of a Packt book, we have a number of things to help you to get the most from your purchase.

Downloading the Example Code for the Book

Visit http://www.packtpub.com/files/code/5524_Code.zip to directly download the example code.

The downloadable files contain instructions on how to use them.

Errata

Although we have taken every care to ensure the accuracy of our contents, mistakes do happen. If you find a mistake in one of our books—maybe a mistake in text or code—we would be grateful if you would report this to us. By doing this you can save other readers from frustration, and help to improve subsequent versions of this book. If you find any errata, report them by visiting http://www.packtpub. com/support, selecting your book, clicking on the **let us know** link, and entering the details of your errata. Once your errata are verified, your submission will be accepted and the errata added to the list of existing errata. The existing errata can be viewed by selecting your title from http://www.packtpub.com/support.

Piracy

Piracy of copyright material on the Internet is an ongoing problem across all media. At Packt, we take the protection of our copyright and licenses very seriously. If you come across any illegal copies of our works in any form on the Internet, please provide the location address or website name immediately so we can pursue a remedy.

Please contact us at copyright@packtpub.com with a link to the suspected pirated material.

We appreciate your help in protecting our authors, and our ability to bring you valuable content.

Questions

You can contact us at questions@packtpub.com if you are having a problem with some aspect of the book, and we will do our best to address it.

1
Introduction to REST

When we look around the Web today, we can see a whole new breed of web applications compared to those available a few years back. It is a whole new Web, and some even call it as Web 2.0. What makes Web 2.0 possible? Web services are one of the key technologies that make the Web as powerful as we can see it is today.

Web services allow heterogeneous systems to communicate with each other using messages. Because the systems could be heterogeneous, the need for interoperability arises. Hence XML is often used to format the messages. Because XML is in text format, almost all systems can understand the messages and work with each other. Messages are used when it comes to communicating between applications that run on different machines. As an example, in a chat application, the text typed in by the users are wrapped in messages, along with the data that would explain where the message should go and how that should be interpreted and passed between the server applications.

There are various technologies that could be used to implement web services. **Representational State Transfer** or **REST** has over time become the preferred technology for web services used in web applications. SOAP web services, also known as **WS-* Stack**, is also a popular alternative. However, there are criticisms against SOAP style services, especially related to the complexity and bulkiness of messages, when it comes to using the services for web applications. Due to the simplicity, ease of use, and the extensive use of web-based technologies such as HTTP that the Web developers are already familiar with, REST has become more popular among web application developers.

This chapter will introduce REST and the concepts related to REST. As a preview, here are the key REST principles to be discussed in this chapter:

- The concept of resource (for example, a document is a resource)
- Every resource given a unique ID (for example, document URL)
- Resources can be related (for example, one document linking to another)
- Use of a standard (HTTP, HTML, XML)

- Resources can have multiple forms (for example, status of a document, updated, validated, deleted)
- Communication in a stateless fashion using HTTP (for example, subsequent requests not related to each other)

Programmable Web

The initial intended use of the Web was to share information among the members of academic research teams. The academicians wanted an easy way to set up and maintain infrastructure to share their findings. They often wanted to link their documents to that of others and previous related work, so they used hyperlinks to site relevant documents.

A useful abstraction of this principle is a document-based hypermedia model that provides content to the users. In the 1990s, Web was used as a platform for distributing information, and it experienced an explosion of users due to the visual appeal of the hypermedia model.

In sync with the ever-increasing number of users, the number of web-based applications too kept up with the pace. With the large number of applications, the volume of data available on the Web has grown tremendously.

With the data available, apart from web applications that could be accessed by users with a web browser, developers built services that could be used by other applications. The programmable Web is the set of enabling technologies that helps developers build services for the Web.

As an example, think of a weather service. More often than not, people who are travelling are interested in weather. So, a travel-related web application could benefit by presenting the users with weather data on the travel website itself. A developer implementing the travel application could consume a weather service to access the weather information and integrate it with the travel application.

RSS (Really Simple Syndication) is a family of Web feed formats used to publish frequently updated contents such as weather information. An RSS document is essentially an XML document. The Yahoo weather service, located at `http://developer.yahoo.com/weather/` provides you with an RSS feed of weather. The following code shows how you can access this code using a few lines of PHP:

```php
<?php
    $url = 'http://weather.yahooapis.com/forecastrss?p=USNY0996';
    $xml = file_get_contents($url);
    echo $xml;
?>
```

This piece of code would fetch the RSS feed that contains the New York weather information. In the above example, the returned XML is just echoed. With a bit of XML processing, you can extract the weather information from the RSS feed returned.

Following is a sample response returned from the service.

```
<?xml version="1.0" encoding="UTF-8" standalone="yes" ?>
<rss version="2.0" xmlns:yweather="http://xml.weather.yahoo.com/ns/
rss/1.0" xmlns:geo="http://www.w3.org/2003/01/geo/wgs84_pos#">
<channel>

<title>Yahoo! Weather - New York, NY</title>
<link>http://us.rd.yahoo.com/dailynews/rss/weather/New_York__NY/
*http://weather.yahoo.com/forecast/USNY0996_f.html</link>
<description>Yahoo! Weather for New York, NY</description>
<language>en-us</language>
<lastBuildDate>Sat, 16 Aug 2008 8:51 am EDT</lastBuildDate>
<ttl>60</ttl>
<yweather:location city="New York" region="NY"   country="US"/>
<yweather:units temperature="F" distance="mi" pressure="in"
speed="mph"/>
<yweather:wind chill="66"   direction="0"   speed="3" />
<yweather:atmosphere humidity="87"  visibility="7"  pressure="30.02"
rising="1" />
<yweather:astronomy sunrise="6:08 am"   sunset="7:52 pm"/>
<image>
<title>Yahoo! Weather</title>
<width>142</width>
<height>18</height>
<link>http://weather.yahoo.com</link>
<url>http://l.yimg.com/us.yimg.com/i/us/nws/th/main_142b.gif</url>
</image>
<item>
<title>Conditions for New York, NY at 8:51 am EDT</title>
<geo:lat>40.67</geo:lat>
<geo:long>-73.94</geo:long>
<link>http://us.rd.yahoo.com/dailynews/rss/weather/New_York__NY/
*http://weather.yahoo.com/forecast/USNY0996_f.html</link>
<pubDate>Sat, 16 Aug 2008 8:51 am EDT</pubDate>
<yweather:condition  text="Fair"  code="34"  temp="66"  date="Sat, 16
Aug 2008 8:51 am EDT" />
<description><![CDATA[
<img src="http://l.yimg.com/us.yimg.com/i/us/we/52/34.gif"/><br />
<b>Current Conditions:</b><br />
Fair, 66 F<BR />
```

```
<BR /><b>Forecast:</b><BR />
Sat - Mostly Sunny. High: 82 Low: 64<br />
Sun - Sunny. High: 88 Low: 67<br />
<br />
<a href="http://us.rd.yahoo.com/dailynews/rss/weather/New_York__NY/
*http://weather.yahoo.com/forecast/USNY0996_f.html">Full Forecast at
Yahoo! Weather</a><BR/>
(provided by The Weather Channel)<br/>
]]></description>
<yweather:forecast day="Sat" date="16 Aug 2008" low="64" high="82"
text="Mostly Sunny" code="34" />
<yweather:forecast day="Sun" date="17 Aug 2008" low="67" high="88"
text="Sunny" code="32" />
<guid isPermaLink="false">USNY0996_2008_08_16_8_51_EDT</guid>
</item>
</channel>
</rss>
```

Here is how you can process the response to print out the temperature:

```
$xml = simplexml_load_string($xml);
    $node = $xml->channel->item;

    $children = $node->children('http://xml.weather.yahoo.com/ns/
                                                   rss/1.0');

    $condition = $children->condition;

    $attributes = $condition->attributes();
    echo $attributes['date'] . " temperature " . $attributes['temp']
                                                   ."F";
```

Technologies such as **AJAX (Asynchronous JavaScript and XML)** help to use web services effectively in web applications. AJAX makes Web applications to become more interactive, faster, and more user-friendly. Since AJAX runs within the web browser itself, and there is information pulled to the web browser, while the user is looking at the currently available content, it helps to yield better user experience. Before AJAX became popular, web browsing was stateless, meaning that the user would have to wait till the next page is loaded and establish a relationship among the contents between the consecutive pages. But with AJAX, users can have a state-full experience, meaning that the next related content would be pulled down to the web browser asynchronously and the effort required to correlate the related content would be minimal. While the user is viewing a web page, an HTTP request could be sent to a server and data could be retrieved in an XML format and a part of the page is updated. As an example, the weather information could be updated in real time without refreshing the whole page, so the user experience is maximized and the web application becomes more appealing to the users.

HTTP and Web Services

Programmable Web uses HTTP as the transportation medium and, most of the time, XML as the message format. In other words, programmable Web could be considered as XML over HTTP. XML is not the only data format available in the programmable Web today. There are a large number of formats available, including HTML, XML, JSON, RSS, Atom, CSV and many other custom formats. Among Web developers, **Plain-Old-XML (POX)** and **JavaScript Object Notation (JSON)** are often popular. Though XML is the most popular message format, JSON also enjoys wide acceptance because it is a lightweight data-interchange format. Human Web is HTML over HTTP and the HTML documents are retrieved from web servers rendered by the web browsers and presented to humans in a visually appealing form. When you browse the Web, you access resources using a **URI (Uniform Resource Indicator)** typed into the address bar of the web browser. The browser uses HTTP GET request and fetches the resources, and the web server will respond with a message filled with the content of the requested resource. Browsers can access a variety of resources using the URIs that include images, videos, and more. Web browsers also use HTTP POST requests to post data filled in by users using forms into web servers. Web servers would process those data and respond accordingly. The HTTP requests can point to URIs that are capable of mapping the request to XML documents representing some forms of data, and those XML documents are processed and the data is consumed by programs.

HTTP is a transport protocol. The HTTP protocol has provisions to represent success or failure status information as well as how the data would be contained in request and response. HTTP by design is a stateless protocol because each request is executed independently, without any knowledge of the requests that came before it.

XML is the data encoding mechanism used in the messages sent. The application-specific data, or in other words, data that relates to business logic would be contained in the XML message.

Let's have a look at an example. Flickr exposes an **Application Programming Interface (API)** that can be used to manage photos http://www.flickr.com/services/api/. There is a test echo API. Please note that you need an API key to use this API and the API documentation given in the aforementioned URL contains details on how to get one. Following is the sample PHP code to access the echo method:

```php
<?php
    $base_url = 'http://api.flickr.com/services/rest/';
    $query_string = '';

    $params = array (
        'method' => 'flickr.test.echo',
```

```
        'name' => 'Sami',
        'api_key' => 'YOUR_API_KEY'
    );

    foreach ($params as $key => $value) {
        $query_string .= "$key=" . urlencode($value) . "&";
    }

    $url = $base_url . "?" . $query_string;
    $client = curl_init($url);
    curl_setopt($client, CURLOPT_RETURNTRANSFER, 1);
    $xml = curl_exec($client);
    curl_close($client);

    echo $xml;
?>
```

 Please remember to replace 'YOUR_API_KEY' with your API key in the above code before you try it.

Let's look at the HTTP request and response exchanged between the server and the client to understand the format of the messages exchanged.

Request:

```
GET /services/rest/?method=flickr.test.echo&name=Sami&api_key=YOUR_
API_KEY& HTTP/1.1
Host: api.flickr.com
```

The above request is a **GET Request**. GET command is immediately followed by the resource location. The resource location that we are accessing is /services/rest/. What follows the location are the parameters. We have three parameters encoded in the request. The method, name, and API key ? character indicates the start of parameters, and parameters are separated from each other using the & character. The final element in the first line of the request is the version of the protocol we are using, in this example HTTP 1.1. The next request header is Host. The resource that we mentioned in the first line is residing on the host api.flickr.com.

Response:

```
HTTP/1.1 200 OK
Date: Mon, 03 Mar 2008 02:44:19 GMT
P3P: policyref="http://p3p.yahoo.com/w3c/p3p.xml", CP="CAO DSP COR CUR
ADM DEV TAI PSA PSD IVAi IVDi CONi TELo OTPi OUR DELi SAMi OTRi UNRi
PUBi IND PHY ONL UNI PUR FIN COM NAV INT DEM CNT STA POL HEA PRE GOV"
Set-Cookie: cookie_l10n=en-us%3Bus; expires=Thursday, 03-Mar-11
02:44:19 GMT; path=/; domain=flickr.com
```

```
Set-Cookie: cookie_intl=deleted; expires=Sunday, 04-Mar-07 02:44:18
GMT; path=/; domain=flickr.com
Content-Length: 167
Cache-Control: private
Vary: Accept-Encoding
Connection: close
Content-Type: text/xml; charset=utf-8

<?xml version="1.0" encoding="utf-8" ?>
<rsp stat="ok">
<method>flickr.test.echo</method>
<name>Sami</name>
<api_key>YOUR_API_KEY</api_key>
</rsp>
```

The first line of the response mentions the HTTP protocol version in use, followed by the status code, indicating the status of the response. In this example, we got a 200 OK, which means that the request we sent resulted in a successful response. Followed by the first line, we can see several lines containing various HTTP headers. The HTTP headers and the response body are separated by an empty line. As you can see, the response body contains an XML document.

In the above example, we accessed a resource via a URI, http://api.flickr.com/services/rest/, and we got back an XML document in response. We just witnessed a web service over HTTP in action. Accessing resources via URIs is one of the key principles behind the REST web services. In fact, in the above example, we used Flickr's REST API.

What is REST?

REST is a software architecture style that can be followed while designing software systems. REST is an ideal design style to be followed for web services based software applications. The principles related to REST were first described by Roy Fielding in his Ph.D. dissertation. You can find the chapter that describes REST in that dissertation here: www.ics.uci.edu/~fielding/pubs/dissertation/rest_arch_style.htm. Following are the key REST principles in brief:

- Provide every resource with a unique ID, for example, a URI
- Link resources with each other, establishing relationships among resources
- Use standard methods (HTTP, media types, XML)
- Resources can have multiple representations that reflect different application states
- The communication should be stateless using the HTTP

Often, REST architectural style is referred to as the architectural style of the Web. Most of today's web applications demonstrate the characteristics of REST architectural style while building services on the Web.

While using REST, a client/server approach is used to separate user interface from data storage. The client/server interaction is stateless and the interactions use a uniform interface.

One of the key elements in the REST architecture is the concept of a resource. Servers host the resources and clients consume those resources. Any information that can be named can be a resource. According to this definition, a document, an image, and today's weather in New York are all examples of resources.

A resource has a resource identifier, a URI, associated with it. In other words, every piece of information has its own URI. This is also a key principle of the Semantic Web, which is an evolving extension of the World Wide Web in which the semantics of information and services on the Web are defined.

A resource can also have an associated representation, a document can be an HTML document, an image can be JPEG binary data and weather data can be represented using an XML document.

A given resource can also have an associated metadata such as media-type and last the modified time. Metadata is useful for consuming a resource. As an example, we can check the last modified time of weather data to see if we have any new updates on weather. We can fetch the resource based on control data that gives an idea on the novelty of the resource. If weather data has not been modified since the last time we fetched it, then there is no point in fetching a new copy of the same old data.

HTTP Methods

Earlier in the section, "HTTP and web services", we discussed the importance of HTTP as a transport protocol for web services. The simplicity and wide adoption in terms of almost all platforms supporting it has made HTTP the superior transportation of the Internet. REST architecture style can benefit from the elements of HTTP by applying REST concepts while implementing applications that run on the Web.

The extensibility and flexibility of the HTTP protocol has contributed a great deal to the success of the Web, and is considered the protocol of the Web today. HTTP protocol can be used to access resources, not only HTML pages, but all types of resources including images, videos, and applications.

When accessing resources with HTTP, a resource identifier is specified along with the action to be performed on that resource. URIs identify the resource. The action to be performed is defined using an HTTP verb. There is a set of HTTP verbs and each verb can have an associated semantics that helps to identify the action to be performed on the resource.

The following table summarizes the HTTP verbs and how they apply while using REST.

Verb	Description
GET	Retrieves a resource identified by a URI.
POST	Sends a resource to the server. Updates the resource in the location identified by the URI.
PUT	Sends a resource to the server, to be stored in the location identified by the URI.
DELETE	Deletes a resource identified by a URI.
HEAD	Retrieves the metadata of a resource identified by the URI.

These HTTP verbs could be viewed in terms of how we can interact with a resource during the life cycle of a resource. PUT creates a resource, and starts the life cycle. GET retrieves the resource and HEAD query for the metadata. POST can be used to update the resource. Even though, in the context of using a web browser, a POST request could have an associated resource returned, in the context of REST, POST should ideally be used for the purpose of updating resources. GET, HEAD and POST can be used to make use of the resource during the lifetime of a resource. DELETE ends the life cycle of a resource. HTTP verbs help to provide a uniform interface for interacting with resources, which is a key principle of REST architectural style.

Let us consider an example. Say, there is a game of football. When a player comes to play, either at the start of the game or as a substitute, we can use PUT verb and create the player resource. This player can have a unique resource identifier, as an example `http://football_game.example.org/game123/player_name`. While the player keeps on playing, POST verb could be used to update the goals scored and the fouls committed by the player resource, and those who access the game information can use the GET operation to access the latest score and committed fouls details for that player resource. When the player gets substituted, DELETE operation could be used to end the player resource life cycle and a new player would replace him/her.

On the Web today, developers mostly use GET and POST, and rarely use PUT and DELETE. One of the key reasons for this situation is the restrictions applied by web servers on these methods. In addition, there are web server modules like the **DAV** module (http://www.webdav.org/mod_dav/) that provides an extension to the HTTP/1.1 protocol that allows clients to perform remote web content authoring operations. This means that in real world applications, developers tend to use POST for creation and deletion operations of resources, in addition to modifications. One of the excuses for not using PUT and DELETE is the fact that firewalls tend to block them. However, it would be good practice to use PUT and DELETE whenever possible rather than overloading POST to implement create and delete. By doing so, you can prevent accidental operations such as deletion of a resource while the user really wanted to update a resource with POST. This makes the API less ambiguous as well. http://www.php.net/manual/en/features.file-upload.put-method.php documents how to make use of the HTTP PUT method.

The Need for RESTful Web Services

As we discussed earlier in this chapter, the advent of services has revolutionized the way web applications are developed and hence the way we use the Web. Out of the web applications we use today, a great majority of applications are written using PHP. Popular applications such as Flickr (http://www.flickr.com/), Wordpress (http://wordpress.com/) and many others are PHP based. According to the TIOBE programming community index [http://www.tiobe.com/index.php/content/paperinfo/tpci/index.html], PHP is the fourth most used programming language and the most used scripting language. Given the wide adoption of PHP and the increasing awareness of REST, it is timely that we look into the ways in which we can do REST with PHP.

By combining the dynamic Web by PHP and mashups by REST and AJAX, we get a new breed of powerful web applications that would drive the future Web to new heights.

Rather than developing all application components in-house, and spending hours on debugging and fixing them, the web services allows us to use proven and tested applications as part of our own application. It is also noteworthy that the volume of data contained within web services and the services available today exposes an enormous volume of data for the taking by the web application developers. If we are building a social networking application and want to add a feature to share photos, we can use the Flickr API and add that functionality rather than writing our own photo sharing application. And the users would be happy because now they can share the photos they have already uploaded, rather than uploading them again, and maintaining the same images at multiple places.

Given the increasing number of services, and the drive towards the REST style architecture for services on the Web, PHP web application developers need to know how to consume REST services, how to build services themselves, and how to design their web applications so that they can reap maximum benefits from REST services for their applications.

REST Tools and Frameworks in PHP

There are many frameworks and tools in PHP that can help users build RESTful applications with ease. To consume services, that is to write clients for existing services, you can start with simple PHP API elements and implement clients. We already saw in some of the samples that were presented earlier in this chapter as to how this can be done.

XML Parsers

Since bulk of the services use XML, XML tools would be handy for both `build` requests and `parse` responses on the client side. On server side too, XML tools are required to do the reverse, to parse the request and build the response.

There are many XML APIs available in PHP, from those, the DOM API and the SimpleXML API are the most popular.

The DOM extension (`http://www.php.net/dom`) allows you to operate on XML documents through the DOM API. The API is fully object-oriented, and adheres to the DOM standards, hence most of the classes are equivalent to those concepts found in DOM specification. It helps to have the DOM standard document available while using this API.

The SimpleXML extension (`http://www.php.net/simplexml`) provides a very simple and easy to use API to work with XML documents in PHP. The PHP object model that could be built out of an XML document using SimpleXML can be processed with normal PHP property selectors and array iterators, making PHP developers' lives much easy when it comes to working with XML constructs using already familiar PHP constructs.

Tools for Accessing Services

For accessing services we need an HTTP client. We can use `file_get_contents` (`http://www.php.net/file_get_contents`) to access not only local files but also those located on remote servers over HTTP. We used this function in the weather sample.

```
$url = 'http://weather.yahooapis.com/forecastrss?p=USNY0996';
$xml = file_get_contents($url);
```

However, `file_get_contents` uses GET, you would need considerable extra work to use a different verb like POST. Also, `fopen` wrappers need to be enabled to let `file_get_contents()` access remote files. System administrators may disable `fopen` wrappers due to security concerns.

The solution to the limitations associated with `file_get_contents` is to use an HTTP client library such as CURL (`http://www.php.net/curl`). CURL PHP API is a wrapper of `libcurl` (`http://curl.haxx.se/libcurl/`), a library that allows you to communicate using many different types of protocols. It supports HTTP verbs such as POST and PUT in addition to GET.

Following code segment shows how to POST some XML data to a URL.

```
$client = curl_init($url);
curl_setopt($client, CURLOPT_RETURNTRANSFER, 1);
// POST XML data with our curl call
curl_setopt($client, CURLOPT_POST, 1);
curl_setopt($client, CURLOPT_POSTFIELDS, $xml_data);
$data = curl_exec($client);
curl_close($client);
```

CURL and `file_get_contents` are the simple PHP API elements that you can use to work with REST style services. CURL is a PHP extension that is required to be loaded in the PHP configuration file `php.ini`. `file_get_contents`, which is only available in PHP versions 4.3 and later. Most of the frameworks that we are going to discuss in the following section provide easy to use client APIs to consume services.

Providing Services

While providing services, you can consider any PHP script hosted with a web server, such as Apache `httpd`, to be a REST style service, because going by the REST principles, the hosted PHP script will have a URI and it will be providing some information to the users who will be accessing it. So it is a resource.

While implementing services that are to be used in the long run and thus maintained, just hosting some PHP scripts and calling them services would not scale. There needs to be some good design principles that we need to adhere to, and we will discuss those later in this book. There are various PHP frameworks that help us build REST style services adhering to good RESTful designing principles. The following section introduces some popular PHP REST frameworks.

PHP REST Frameworks

The following table lists some PHP frameworks that help you build REST style applications.

Framework or Tool	URL
Tonic	http://tonic.sourceforge.net/
Konstrukt	http://www.konstrukt.dk/
Zend Framework	http://framework.zend.com/manual/en/zend.rest.html
WSO2 WSF/PHP	http://wso2.org/projects/wsf/php
Madeam	http://madeam.com/
dbscript	http://dbscript.net/

Tonic

Tonic is an open-source RESTFul web application development PHP library. It is designed so that the user can build RESTFul applications in the correct way. The concept of resources are given due prominence, and the library gives the developer the liberty to go about designing the application.

Konstrukt

Konstrukt is a RESTFul framework of controllers for PHP5. The controllers are resources and the URI-to-controller mapping gives the application a logical structure. The framework exposes the HTTP methods to the developer and enables the developer to customize the application the way he or she wants.

Zend Framework

The Zend Framework provides both client and server APIs to deal with REST services and clients. `Zend_Rest_Server` is the class that you can use to provide REST style services. `Zend_Rest_Client` class can be used to consume REST style services. The `Server` class is capable of exposing functions and classes using a meaningful and simple XML format. When accessing these services using the `Client` class, it is possible to retrieve the return data from the remote call easily. The `Client` class can also be used to consume services that do not use `Zend_Rest_Server` class to implement the services.

WSO2 WSF/PHP

WSO2 web services framework for PHP has comprehensive support for REST style services and clients. You can both provide and consume services using REST principles. `WSService` and `WSClient` classes can be used on server side and client side respectively. The advantage of this framework is that a given service can be exposed both as a REST service as well as a SOAP service simultaneously.

Madeam

Madeam is a rapid application development PHP Framework based on **MVC (Model-View-Controller)** principle. It allows quick prototyping and deployment of web applications and includes support for building REST style applications.

dbscript

dbscript is a Web development framework. Key features of this framework include RESTful handling of URLs, HTTP style controllers, and support for Atom over HTTP.

What Framework to Use

Given the number of frameworks available, it would be a challenge to make a choice. As always, selecting one from the many alternatives available has to be based on the requirements of the application to be developed.

Tonic helps to adhere to correct REST principles, but may lack maturity as compared to a framework like the Zend Framework. The same applies to Konstrukt.

Zend Framework is a very mature framework and in addition to REST support, it is equipped with a very useful set of PHP library APIs that would come in handy while developing PHP applications.

WSO2 WSF/PHP would be a good choice if there is a need to make use of advanced web services, especially SOAP based web services alongside REST style services. WSO2 WSF/PHP provides an easy mapping from application design to implementation, when it comes to REST style applications.

Madeam would be ideal for applications adhering to a Model-View-Controller (MVC) design principle. However, note that, while developing REST style applications, more than the presentation, that is the View, we are more interested in resource design.

One of the noteworthy attributes of dbscript is its built-in capabilities to handle feed formats such as Atom.

For complete novices, it would be advisable to start with the Zend Framework and then move on to WSO2 WSF/PHP because Zend framework has an easy to use API for simple services and clients and once there is a good understanding on the principles one can move on to the WSO2 WSF/PHP, which has provision for advance use.

Summary

This chapter introduced the concepts related to programmable Web, showed how HTTP and web services are related to each other, introduced the principles behind REST, explained how HTTP verbs are used in REST applications, explained the need for RESTFul web services while building PHP web applications, and introduced some frameworks and tools that can be used to work with REST in PHP.

REST is an architectural style with the concept of resource at its heart and with which we can build web services. REST principles can be applied with HTTP to build powerful services for the Web.

In this chapter, we also saw some bits and pieces of PHP code that can be used to access REST services that are publicly available. By now, you should have a general understanding of what REST is all about. In the next chapter, we will look into how PHP can be used to consume public REST style services in a bit more detail.

2
REST with PHP—
A First Look

This chapter will introduce the basic PHP routines that could be used to work with REST. We will cover the areas related to:

- Building a request
- Sending the request
- Receiving the response and processing the received response
- How to work with HTTP verbs using an HTTP client library like CURL for sending and receiving messages
- How to use XML parser APIs in PHP to build and process XML requests and responses
    - Build requests on client side
    - Build responses on server side
    - Process responses on client side
    - Process requests on server side

HTTP with PHP

There are multiple techniques and libraries available with PHP to deal with HTTP. In this book, our main interest would be on the mechanisms of dealing with HTTP that would help us use REST.

As mentioned in the previous chapter, if you host a PHP script with a web server that becomes a resource as per the principles of REST architectural style, then you have a service. So, when you use a web server, you have the luxury of the web server dealing with the HTTP protocol for you. You have little to worry about other than being sensitive to the elements of the protocol such as the verbs in use.

If you are implementing service clients, then you have to use some form of HTTP client library that will help you in using various HTTP verbs and other protocol elements with ease.

Let us start with the simplest cases. As briefly shown in the previous chapter, `file_get_contents` can be used to access a resource over the HTTP protocol.

```php
<?php
$url = "http://search.yahooapis.com/WebSearchService/V1/spellingSugges
tion?appid=YahooDemo&query=apocalipto";
$result = file_get_contents($url);
echo $result;
?>
```

The output that we get after running the code snippet is as follows.

```xml
<?xml version="1.0" encoding="UTF-8" ?>
- <ResultSet xmlns:xsi="http://www.w3.org/2001/XMLSchema-instance"
xmlns="urn:yahoo:srch" xsi:schemaLocation="urn:yahoo:srch http://api.
search.yahoo.com/WebSearchService/V1/WebSearchSpellingResponse.xsd">
  <Result>apocalypto</Result>
  </ResultSet>
```

In this sample, we are accessing the Yahoo spelling suggestion service. While using the `file_get_contents` method would be simple, there are a few limitations in using this function to access service. As an example, this function would always use HTTP GET method on the given URL. You have no control over the HTTP method to be used with this function. Also note that `file_put_contents` does not support writing to network connections, hence you would not be able to perform a PUT operation on a resource with that function. Also note that this function may not be enabled in most hosting platforms, because of `safe_mode` (http://www.php.net/features.safe-mode).

So we need a more feature-packed HTTP client library. As we have already seen in the last chapter, we can use the CURL PHP API (http://www.php.net/curl).

CURL

CURL is an abbreviation for "**Client URL Request Library**", or sometimes the recursive version "**Curl URL Request Library**". CURL is a powerful library because of the power of the library that it wraps, namely `libcurl`. The reasons for `libcurl` to be considered a powerful library include the fact that it currently supports the `http`, `https`, `ftp`, `gopher`, `telnet`, `dict`, `file`, and `ldap` protocols, its support for HTTPS certificates, HTTP POST, HTTP PUT, FTP uploading, HTTP form based upload, proxies, cookies, and username password authentication. CURL PHP API comes with a wide array of options and features. This allows users to fine tune the requests and the way that the responses are handled.

In this section, we will explore how we can utilize CURL to use various HTTP methods that we would require to consume REST services. Note that CURL is a PHP extension. Usually it comes pre-built with the binary distributions. However, on shared Web hosting environments, `libcurl` might often not be available since PHP extensions are reduced to a bare minimum. And if you want to install PHP5 by building it from source distribution, CURL is not enabled by default compilation configuration. You can find more install and configuration options at `http://us.php.net/manual/en/curl.setup.php`.

There are four main steps when you are using CURL:

1. Initialize CURL
2. Set options
3. Execute CURL
4. Close CURL

These steps, initializing, executing, and closing are standard steps that you would use irrespective of the HTTP method that you want to use with the URL. It is the set of options that you have to change based on the HTTP method you want to use. As an example, CURLOPT_GET option would be used for HTTP GET and CURLOPT_POST would be used for HTTP POST.

Initialize:

```
$ch = curl_init();
```

Set Options:

```
curl_setopt($ch, CURLOPT_URL, $url);
curl_setopt($ch, CURLOPT_GET, true);
```

Execute:

```
curl_exec($ch);
```

Close:

```
curl_close($ch);
```

In this example, we are using HTTP GET method. We tell CURL to use GET method by setting CURLOPT_GET option to true.

HTTP GET

It is useful to know what to expect when you are using various HTTP verbs. This is because you can always look into the sent message and verify that the correct HTTP verb was used along with parameters. As an example, have a look at the following message:

```
GET /WebSearchService/V1/spellingSuggestion?appid=YahooDemo&query=apoc
alipto HTTP/1.0
Host: search.yahooapis.com:80
```

It shows that a GET request has been sent to `search.yahooapis.com` host, requesting for the resource that provides spell suggestion functionality. You can also note the fact that we are using the HTTP 1.0 protocol version here. You will find more information on how to capture the messages and verify the integrity of messages in Chapter 6, Troubleshooting Services and Clients.

Earlier in this chapter it was shown how to access the Yahoo spelling service with the `file_get_contents` function. The following code shows how to do the same with CURL. As you will notice, the code is a bit lengthier than the equivalent `file_get_contents` version. Obviously, this is the cost you have to pay in exchange of the customizability of CURL. However, you will soon realize that the increased number of lines is negligible in comparison to what you can do with CURL.

```php
<?php
$url = "http://search.yahooapis.com/WebSearchService/V1/spellingSugges
tion?appid=YahooDemo&query=apocalipto";

$ch = curl_init();

curl_setopt($ch, CURLOPT_URL, $url);
curl_setopt($ch, CURLOPT_GET, true);

curl_exec($ch);
curl_close($ch);
?>
```

The code shown above would result in a request that looks like the following. (Note that these messages were captured using a message capturing tool, explained in Chapter 6).

```
GET /WebSearchService/V1/spellingSuggestion?appid=YahooDemo&query=apoc
alipto HTTP/1.0
Host: search.yahooapis.com:80
```

And the response:

```
HTTP/1.1 200 OK
Date: Sat, 17 May 2008 01:24:27 GMT
Cache-Control: private
```

```
Connection: close
Content-Type: text/xml; charset=utf-8
<?xml version="1.0" encoding="UTF-8"?>
    <ResultSet xmlns:xsi="http://www.w3.org/2001/XMLSchema-instance"
xmlns="urn:yahoo:srch" xsi:schemaLocation="urn:yahoo:srch http://api.
search.yahoo.com/WebSearchService/V1/WebSearchSpellingResponse.xsd">
        <Result>apocalypto</Result>
    </ResultSet>
```

When you run into trouble and want to troubleshoot to figure out what went wrong, looking into the messages to verify the verbs, parameters, HTTP headers and the message content, usually termed payload, would be very helpful. In the following sections, sample source code will be presented to demonstrate how to use CURL API for PHP to make use of various HTTP verbs.

Also, it is worth mentioning that this script would print the response from the service directly to the console, even though we are not using an echo in the script. This is because we need one more option to instruct CURL not to send the received data to the standard output. That option is named CURLOPT_RETURNTRANSFER and must be set to true to get the result of the CURL invocation as a string to a variable. When using CURL for REST clients, more often than not, you would want to capture the return value to a variable rather than printing it directly as an output, because you often would want to process the response from the service before presenting that to the user.

Here is the same client code with option CURLOPT_RETURNTRANSFER set to true. Note that unlike in the previous sample, we now have to use echo to display the returned XML response, and in order to echo we need to capture the response returned as a string from the curl_exec function. Also note that in this sample we are not looking to process the response, rather the output as it is. Later in this chapter we will discuss how to use XML parsers to process the response.

```php
<?php
$url = "http://search.yahooapis.com/WebSearchService/V1/spellingSugges
tion?appid=YahooDemo&query=apocalipto";

$ch = curl_init();

curl_setopt($ch, CURLOPT_URL, $url);
curl_setopt($ch, CURLOPT_RETURNTRANSFER, true);
curl_setopt($ch, CURLOPT_GET, true);

$response = curl_exec($ch);

curl_close($ch);

echo $response;
?>
```

HTTP POST

Most of the services on the internet that support POST or PUT operations would require some form of authentication. This is due to the sensitive nature of these operations especially when it comes to security. The service providers need to control those people who can modify resources.

Because of the complexity of some of the authentication methods in use, if we use a public service to demonstrate the POST method, it would reduce the prominence that should be given to the main subject in discussion in this section of the chapter. Hence, let us use our own service script to see how to use HTTP methods such as POST, PUT and DELETE.

Following is a simple PHP script that you can deploy with your web server and can act as our test service.

```php
<?php
$input = file_get_contents("php://input");
file_put_contents("php://output", $input);
?>
```

This service script is very simple and straightforward. We just read the incoming payload and write that to the output, a very simple echo service. We will focus on the client side, making requests and processing responses, for the time being, rather than handling requests and generating responses on the server side. We shall visit the server side later. To keep things clean, let's deploy this service to a folder named rest/02 on the web server and you can name this script message_trace.php. To deploy the service, create a directory structure rest/02 in the document root directory of the server and create a PHP script message_service. php in the 02 directory. Copy the PHP script in the previous listing to the message_service.php file.

Now let's see how to write a PHP client that will POST data to this service. This client would send the payload to the service, and the service would echo that payload back. The client would capture the response and echo the response to the output. And here is code for the client.

```php
<?php
$url = 'http://localhost/rest/02/message_trace.php';

$data = <<<XML
<text>Hello World!</text>
XML;

$ch = curl_init();

curl_setopt($ch, CURLOPT_URL, $url);
```

```
curl_setopt($ch, CURLOPT_RETURNTRANSFER, true);
curl_setopt($ch, CURLOPT_POST, true);
curl_setopt($ch, CURLOPT_POSTFIELDS, $data);

$response = curl_exec($ch);

curl_close($ch);

echo $response;
?>
```

The output would be:

```
<text>Hello World!</text>
```

First, the URL where the service is located is defined. We assume that the server is the localhost, meaning that the service script is hosted on the same machine where the client is hosted.

```
$url = 'http://localhost/rest/02/message_trace.php';
```

Then the message content and the payload to be sent to the server is defined.

```
$data = <<<XML
<text>Hello World!</text>
XML;
```

Then the initialization and the setting of options for CURL are done.

```
$ch = curl_init();
curl_setopt($ch, CURLOPT_URL, $url);
curl_setopt($ch, CURLOPT_RETURNTRANSFER, true);
```

Set the option to indicate that we want to make use of HTTP POST verb.

```
curl_setopt($ch, CURLOPT_POST, true);
```

Also, set the data to be posted as an option.

```
curl_setopt($ch, CURLOPT_POSTFIELDS, $data);
```

If you compare this script that POST data from a service to the earlier script where we GET data from a service, you can notice some minor differences.

- Unlike in the GET case, we have some $data prepared to be sent to the service
- We have used CURLOPT_POST instead of CURLOPT_GET
- And we also have used a new option CURLOPT_POSTFIELDS

The rest of the code is similar to the GET client, since we follow the four step process for using CURL.

The semantics of this script is very simple: Prepare the data to be posted, set the HTTP method to be used to POST, set the option pointing to the data to be POSTed, send the request that is POST data, and process the response.

In the REST architectural style, POST is used to update a resource and the response might not contain any payload. However, some applications could choose to return the old resource value in the response after updating the resource with new incoming data.

HTTP PUT

As in the case of the example used to demonstrate HTTP POST method, we will use a simple demo service for demonstrating HTTP PUT method, to keep our focus on how to use CURL to make a PUT request. Here is the code for service script, and we will name this script as put.php.

```php
<?php
$putdata = fopen("php://input", "r");
$fp = fopen("put_data_file.txt", "a");
while ($data = fread($putdata, 1024))
  fwrite($fp, $data);
fclose($fp);
fclose($putdata);
?>
```

This simple script will open the input stream containing the PUT data as a file. A file, when read from start to end could be considered as a stream of data. A file could be opened and its data read, and that data could be considered as an input for a script. Since this mechanism provides the input as a stream of data, it is often termed as the input stream. Similarly, a file could be opened and the output be written to that file, then we call it the output stream. After reading the input stream, this script then opens another file named put_data_file.txt and places all the data PUT into that file. Lets host this service in the folder rest/02.

Note that, even though in theory we could create a new resource with HTTP PUT method with REST architectural style, most of the web servers will not allow the creation of new resources on the server due to security reasons. Since PHP is often hosted as a module of the web server, the file write privileges the PHP script has would be similar to those of the web server. Web servers discourage the Web application users by allowing them to place content into the web server host's file system, because such facilities could be misused to upload harmful scripts and compromise the host machine's security by executing those uploaded scripts.

```php
<?php
$url = 'http://localhost/rest/02/put.php';
$fh = fopen('data.txt', 'r');
```

```php
$data = file_get_contents('data.txt');
$ch = curl_init();
curl_setopt($ch, CURLOPT_URL, $url);
curl_setopt($ch, CURLOPT_PUT, true);
curl_setopt($ch, CURLOPT_INFILE, $fh);
curl_setopt($ch, CURLOPT_INFILESIZE, strlen($data));
curl_exec($ch);
curl_close($ch);
?>
```

To run the previous PHP script, create an input text file data.txt, which has some text data in the document root directory of the server.

Note that there is no output generated by this example script. This is because the script uses the functionality provided by the script that it is accessing, namely put.php, the service in this case, and there is no response message involved with this interaction. When working with services and clients, it is a common scenario to have no visible output associated with the client and server interactions. The client would trigger some business processing on the server side, and the service would consume the request and do the needful backend processing, and would not have anything to return to the client.

You can see from this source, the PUT script is very similar to the POST script, except for a few differences. One trivial change from POST to PUT is that the option CURLOPT_PUT instead of CURLOPT_POST has been used. Also, unlike in the POST case, where we set the post data using CURLOPT_POSTFIELDS option, we have set the CURLOPT_INFILE and CURLOPT_INFILESIZE options to provide the name of the file and the size of the data in the file to be PUT.

HTTP DELETE

HTTP DELETE verb is also a sensitive verb like HTTP PUT. This is because the verb can be used to delete a resource, and deleting an existing resource requires proper access privileges. For demonstration purposes, we will use the same service script that we used for PUT operation and see how CURL API can be used to invoke HTTP DELETE. Here is the source code.

```php
<?php
$url = 'http://localhost/rest/02/put.php';
$ch = curl_init();
curl_setopt($ch, CURLOPT_URL, $url);
curl_setopt($ch, CURLOPT_CUSTOMREQUEST, "DELETE");
curl_exec($ch);
curl_close($ch);
?>
```

As you may notice, unlike the POST or PUT requests, there is no dedicated option in CURL for delete. Rather you have to use the CURLOPT_CUSTOMREQUEST option with the value DELETE to use the DELETE verb. Also note that, in this simple example, when the put.php script received the DELETE request, the script would simply ignore the request, and leave the data file content as it is. Alternatively, the service script could have erased the data file.

```
unlink("put_data_file.txt");
```

One of the common uses of the HTTP DELETE operation is to end the life of a resource, as we discussed in the last chapter. As an example, you could delete a database entry mapped to a resource after receiving a DELETE request. We will see this later in this book, in Chapter 4 where we will discuss a real world sample application.

Building the Request with XML Tools

Primary use of web services will be with XML message format. Of course other messaging formats could be used, however, for the purpose of interoperability XML is the preferred format. Before sending a request from a client to a service, we have to build the request message in XML and hand it over to the HTTP transport. While sending the response to the client, the service too needs to build the response in XML. So the same techniques used for building the request on client side could be used to build the response on the service side.

PHP comes with a number of XML parsers, some built-in and some third-party. For almost all common use cases the built-in parser APIs that come with PHP are sufficient.

The two main XML APIs in PHP are the SimpleXML extension (http://www.php. net/manual/en/book.simplexml.php) and the DOM extension (http://www.php. net/manual/en/book.dom.php). Both these XML APIs come with PHP 5 and they are built-in by default, meaning there are no additional installation steps to enable them. Both of them are based on libxml XML parser (http://www.xmlsoft.org/). Since they are based on libxml, which is a parser written in C, these PHP parser APIs yield high performance while processing XML.

While using XML parsers there are two main modes of operation. One is to build the XML structure that we want, either to write that to a file or to send that over the network. The other mode of operation is to parse XML that is read from a file or from a received stream over a network interface. Reading an XML stream from a file or a network interface and building an equivalent XML object structure in PHP (or any other programming language) is termed as de-serialization. Writing an XML stream to a file or a network interface from an XML object structure is termed as serialization.

Coming back to the topic of building the request, we must build the XML object tree using some PHP code and serialize that object tree to get the string representation of the XML object tree.

SimpleXML

The most simple way to build an XML payload with SimpleXML is to use the XML string and pass it to the `SimpleXMLElement` constructor. However, for most of the dynamic applications we should be able to form the request payload on the fly. Hence we cannot always assume the luxury of pre-defined knowledge on what the content of the XML payload would be. However, it is reasonable to assume that all applications would have some knowledge of the overall structure of the XML payload to be sent in the request.

```php
<?php
$xmlstr = <<<XML
<books>
    <book>
        <title/>
    </book>
</books>
XML;
$xml = new SimpleXMLElement($xmlstr);
$book = $xml->book[0];
$book->addAttribute('type', 'Computer');
$book->title = 'RESTful Web Services!';
$author = $xml->book[0]->addChild('author');
$author->addChild('name', 'Sami');
echo $xml->asXML();
?>
```

In the above example, first an XML template is defined with the variable `$xmlstr`. The variable is initialized to contain a valid XML string, however it does not have any useful content to start with. So we are first defining a structure for the XML message using a simple string and then we add the content programmatically. The output from the previous script is **'Sami'**.

Next, a `SimpleXMLElement` instance is created with the XML string that was defined. With the above source code, the XML structure that we want to build is as follows:

```
<books>
  <book type="Computer">
    <title>PHP Web Services</title>
    <author><name>Sami</name></author>
  </book>
</books>
```

So starting from the initial template XML structure, the first thing we have to do is to add the type attribute to the book element with the value `Computer`. Basically, with this attribute we want to express that the type of book is `Computer`. To do this, first we access the first book element in the XML template. This is done with this line:

```
$book = $xml->book[0];
```

The array notation with the index 0 means that we want the first element. In fact, there is only one book element in the template. However, we still have to use the indexing mechanism because in an XML document it is quite possible to have more than one element with the same name and the PHP API uses the indexing mechanism to cater for that situation. The `addAttribute` method is used to add the attribute to the desired element.

```
$book->addAttribute('type', 'Computer');
```

The second important operation done in this source code is setting the title text to `PHP Web Services`. This can be done by setting the title element of the PHP array structure element with the name `book` to the desired text. The title array element is accessed using `$book->title` operation.

```
$book->title = 'RESTful Web Services!';
```

The next section of the code adds two elements. `author` is the parent element and `name` is the child element, and the child consists of text "Sami". The `author` element is added to the book element and the `name` is added to the `author` element. The `addChild()` method is used to get the job done.

```
$author = $xml->book[0]->addChild('author');
$author->addChild('name', 'Sami');
```

The final step in the code that is the call to the operation as `XML()` serializes the XML object tree that we build.

DOM

DOM API is another XML API available in PHP that is built-in. The following source code will build the same XML tree that we saw in the previous section using the DOM API.

```
<?php
$xmlstr = <<<XML
<books>
    <book>
        <title/>
    </book>
```

```
    </books>
    XML;

    $doc = new DOMDocument;
    $doc->preserveWhiteSpace = false;
    $doc->loadXML($xmlstr);

    $books = $doc->getElementsByTagName('book');
    $books->item(0)->setAttribute('type', 'Computer');

    $books->item(0)->childNodes->item(0)->nodeValue = 'RESTful Web
    Services';

    $author_node = $doc->createElement('author');
    $books->item(0)->appendChild($author_node);

    $name_node = $doc->createElement('name');
    $name_node->nodeValue = 'Sami';
    $author_node->appendChild($name_node);

    echo $doc->saveXML();
    ?>
```

Comparatively this source code is a bit lengthier compared to the SimpleXML based source code doing the identical job. However, it must be noted that the DOM API is much more comprehensive and feature-rich compared to the SimpleXML API. You can get a feel of this if you compare the API documentation of the two APIs. (The links to the API documents were given earlier in this chapter.)

Processing the Response

Once the response is received, the client needs to de-serialize the response XML message received from the service. The service too needs to de-serialize the incoming request received from the client. In the previous section we saw how to build the XML tree. In this section we will explore how to parse an XML document and then traverse that parsed XML tree.

SimpleXML

Let's look at how to use the SimpleXML API to parse an XML document. In this section, we will use a file named book.xml with the following content.

```
<?xml version="1.0"?>
<books>
  <book type="Computer">
    <title>PHP Web Services</title>
    <author><name>Sami</name></author>
  </book>
</books>
```

Note that this XML is the same as the XML structure that we had built in the previous section. The only difference is that we are going to read and traverse the XML tree rather than trying to build the XML tree.

```php
<?php
$xml = simplexml_load_file('book.xml');
$book = $xml->book[0];

echo "Book title : " . $book->title ."\n";
echo "Book author name : " . $book->author->name ."\n";
$attributes = $book->attributes();
echo "Book type : " . $attributes['type'] ."\n";
?>
```

In this code, we first load the book.xml file from the file system.

```php
$xml = simplexml_load_file('book.xml');
```

Then we access the first element in the XML file with the name book.

```php
$book = $xml->book[0];
```

And then we access the book information and display those.

```php
echo "Book title : " . $book->title ."\n";
echo "Book author name : " . $book->author->name ."\n";
$attributes = $book->attributes();
echo "Book type : " . $attributes['type'] ."\n";
```

DOM

Let's see how we can parse the same XML file and traverse the XML tree using the DOM API.

```php
<?php
$doc = new DOMDocument;
$doc->preserveWhiteSpace = false;
$doc->load('book.xml');

$books = $doc->getElementsByTagName('book');
echo "Book title : " . $books->item(0)->childNodes->item(0)->nodeValue
."\n";
echo "Book author name : " . $books->item(0)->childNodes->item(1)-
>nodeValue ."\n";

echo "Book type : " . $books->item(0)->getAttribute('type')."\n";
?>
```

In this code, we first create a `DOMDocument` instance and set the `preserveWhiteSpace` option to `false`. What this means is that the parser should remove the redundant white spaces present between the elements while parsing the XML document. The next step in the source code is to load the `book.xml` file form the file system.

```
$doc->load('book.xml');
```

Then we access the set of elements in the XML file with the name `book`.

```
$books = $doc->getElementsByTagName('book');
```

Of course there is only one `book` element in the document, but as explained earlier, the parser provides an array notation in the API to accommodate the possibility of the presence of multiple elements with the same name.

Next we access the `title` and `author name` elements.

```
echo "Book title : " . $books->item(0)->childNodes->item(0)->nodeValue
."\n";
echo "Book author name : " . $books->item(0)->childNodes->item(1)-
>nodeValue ."\n";
```

Finally the `getAttribute()` method is used to access the `type` attribute.

```
echo "Book type : " . $books->item(0)->getAttribute('type')."\n";
```

If you run the SimpleXML based PHP script and the DOM API based PHP script given in the above section, you will get identical output on the console.

Consuming Flickr

In this section, we will use the HTTP client libraries and an XML parser API to consume the Flickr REST API. Flickr is a popular web-based application that allows you to share your photos on the Internet. The Flickr API consists of a set of callable methods and some API endpoints that allows developers to use the Flickr services by integrating Flickr to their applications. To perform an action using the Flickr API, you need to select the relevant operation from the API, send a request to its endpoint specifying a method and some arguments and then you will receive a formatted response.

Note that you have to get a Flickr API key for yourself to run the samples given in this section. Details on how to get a Flickr API key can be found at `http://www.flickr.com/services/api/misc.api_keys.html`.

First let's use a simple API call to get familiar with the concepts related to the Flickr API. In this first sample we will search for a Flickr user by name.

The complete Flickr API can be found on the URL http://www.flickr.com/services/api/. Out of this, we will use the method call findByUsername. The documentation for this method could be found at http://www.flickr.com/services/api/flickr.people.findByUsername.html.

```php
<?php
$base_url = 'http://api.flickr.com/services/rest/';
$query_string = '';
$params = array (
  'method' => 'flickr.people.findByUsername',
  'api_key' => 'YOUR_API_KEY',
  'username' => 'Sami'
);
$query_string = http_build_query($params);
$url = $base_url . '?' . $query_string;
$client = curl_init($url);
curl_setopt($client, CURLOPT_RETURNTRANSFER, 1);
$response = curl_exec($client);
curl_close($client);
$xml = simplexml_load_string($response);
foreach ($xml->user as $user) {
  $attributes = $user->attributes();
  echo 'User ID : ' . $attributes['id'] . "\n";
  echo 'User NSID : ' . $attributes['nsid'] . "\n";
}
?>
```

The $base_url variable is assigned to the base REST URL where Flickr expects all REST requests would be sent to. Each and every operation has an array of request parameters. Details on the request parameters required by a Flickr method call can be found on the respective API documentation page.

All Flickr method calls expect two mandatory parameters in the request:

- The method name
- The API key

The first two elements of the $params array represent those two parameters. The third parameter is specific to the operation that we are going to invoke, namely findByUsername.

```php
$params = array (
  'method' => 'flickr.people.findByUsername',
  'api_key' => 'YOUR_API_KEY',
  'username' => 'Sami'
);
```

Note that, in order to run this PHP script you have to get a Flickr API key for yourself, and replace "YOUR_API_KEY" string with your own API key. Details on how to get a Flickr API key can be found at http://www.flickr.com/services/api/misc.api_keys.html.

In this example, we are going to search for a user named Sami. Hence we set the username parameter in the $params array to that value.

After defining the parameter array, the next step is to append the parameter key value pairs to the request URL. In other words, we have to build a request query string using the parameter array. This is done using a http_build_query function.

Once the query parameter string is formed with the parameters, it is joined with the base URL to form the final URL string. It is this URL string where base URL plus the query parameters are passed to CURL. For this example the final URL will look something like:

```
http://api.flickr.com/services/rest/?method=flickr.people.
findByUsername&api_key=your_api_key&username=Sami&
```

With the above URL, we access the service using PHP CURL API and the received response is captured to the $response variable. Then that response is passed to the XML parser. SimpleXML API is used in this sample to parse the response. From the API document it is known that the response would be of the following format.

```
<rsp stat="ok">
    <user id="12037949632@N01" nsid="12037949632@N01">
        <username>Stewart</username>
    </user>
</rsp>
```

In sync with the expected format of the response this example script prints out the user ID and NSID received in the response as shown below:

```
User ID : 48600079231@N01 User NSID : 48600079231@N01
```

Photo Search

Now that we are familiar with the Flickr REST API, let's see how to use image search API to find images with a search term.

```php
<?php
$base_url = 'http://api.flickr.com/services/rest/';
$query_string = '';

$params = array (
  'method' => 'flickr.photos.search',
```

```php
    'api_key' => 'YOUR_API_KEY',
    'tags' => 'flowers',
    'per_page' => 10
);

$query_string = http_build_query($params);

$url = $base_url . '?' . $query_string;

$client = curl_init($url);
curl_setopt($client, CURLOPT_RETURNTRANSFER, 1);
$response = curl_exec($client);
curl_close($client);

$xml = simplexml_load_string($response);

foreach ($xml->photos->photo as $photo) {
  $attributes = $photo->attributes();
  $image_url = 'http://farm' . $attributes['farm'] . '.static.flickr.
com/' . $attributes['server'] . '/' . $attributes['id'] . '_' .
$attributes['secret'] . '.jpg';
  echo "<img src='" . $image_url . "'/>";
}
?>
```

The output from the script is shown below:

This example is quite similar to the previous user search sample. We set the query parameters like in case of the user search: first two are the method name and the API key respectively. Then we set the parameters that are specific to the photo search. We are going to search for the term 'flowers' in photo tags. The per_page parameter is set to 10, meaning we are expecting 10 search results per page.

The XML response from Flickr would be as shown below:

```
<?xml version="1.0" encoding="utf-8" ?>
<rsp stat="ok">
<photos page="1" pages="222761" perpage="10" total="2227604">
        <photo id="2426964909" owner="15366215@N00"
secret="53a301dc73" server="3019" farm="4" title="rocio 2 20Apr08
Stansted Airport" ispublic="1" isfriend="0
" isfamily="0" />
        <photo id="2427778480" owner="92329419@N00"
secret="8edeff5d1c" server="3110" farm="4" title="P1020588"
ispublic="1" isfriend="0" isfamily="0" />
        <photo id="2426968511" owner="92329419@N00"
secret="23ecee7e0d" server="2201" farm="3" title="P1020595"
ispublic="1" isfriend="0" isfamily="0" />
        <photo id="2427782016" owner="92329419@N00"
secret="53d1c19c19" server="2136" farm="3" title="P1020592"
ispublic="1" isfriend="0" isfamily="0" />
        <photo id="2426971113" owner="92329419@N00"
secret="55ff6a4ab5" server="3263" farm="4" title="P1020599"
ispublic="1" isfriend="0" isfamily="0" />
        <photo id="2426962095" owner="23913224@N08"
secret="d7f09ccf14" server="2417" farm="3" title="Petunia Flowers"
ispublic="1" isfriend="0" isfamily="0" />
        <photo id="2427775060" owner="23913224@N08"
secret="ff84f68c5e" server="3002" farm="4" title="IMG_6668"
ispublic="1" isfriend="0" isfamily="0" />
        <photo id="2426970287" owner="92329419@N00"
secret="df75b2cb3d" server="3202" farm="4" title="P1020596"
ispublic="1" isfriend="0" isfamily="0" />
        <photo id="2426961859" owner="23913224@N08"
secret="68391f48dc" server="3136" farm="4" title="Petunia in Bahrain"
ispublic="1" isfriend="0" isfamily="0"
 />
        <photo id="2427778762" owner="15366215@N00"
secret="d9b82cfa07" server="2205" farm="3" title="rocio 1
20Apr08,Stansted airport" ispublic="1" isfriend="0
" isfamily="0" />
</photos>
</rsp>
```

There are other optional parameters that could be used while doing photo search. Details of the complete photo search API could be found at
`http://www.flickr.com/services/api/flickr.photos.search.html`.

Once we have built the query parameters and sent the request to Flickr using CURL API and got the response, we pass that response to the XML parser.

For each photo element in the response, we build the image URL in the sample PHP script. Information on how to extract the real image URL from the response returned is documented at `http://www.flickr.com/services/api/misc.urls.html`.

The output from this PHP script would look as follows::

```
<img src='http://farm4.static.flickr.com/3019/2426964909_53a301dc73.
jpg'/>
<img src='http://farm4.static.flickr.com/3110/2427778480_8edeff5d1c.
jpg'/>
<img src='http://farm3.static.flickr.com/2201/2426968511_23ecee7e0d.
jpg'/>
<img src='http://farm3.static.flickr.com/2136/2427782016_53d1c19c19.
jpg'/>
<img src='http://farm4.static.flickr.com/3263/2426971113_55ff6a4ab5.
jpg'/>
<img src='http://farm3.static.flickr.com/2417/2426962095_d7f09ccf14.
jpg'/>
<img src='http://farm4.static.flickr.com/3002/2427775060_ff84f68c5e.
jpg'/>
<img src='http://farm4.static.flickr.com/3202/2426970287_df75b2cb3d.
jpg'/>
<img src='http://farm4.static.flickr.com/3136/2426961859_68391f48dc.
jpg'/>
<img src='http://farm3.static.flickr.com/2205/2427778762_d9b82cfa07.
jpg'/>
```

You can view this with a browser and see the photos corresponding to the search displayed.

Here is a sample output from this script:

Photo Search with Information

Let's extend the photo search example to include more image information. In this example, we will first do a photo search like we did in the previous PHP script and, for each result, get more information such as image tags and web page URL for the image.

```php
<?php
$base_url = 'http://api.flickr.com/services/rest/';
$query_string = '';

$params = array (
    'method' => 'flickr.photos.search',
    'api_key' => 'YOUR_API_KEY',
```

```php
    'tags' => 'flowers',
    'per_page' => 10
);

$query_string = http_build_query($params);

$url = "$base_url?$query_string";

$client = curl_init($url);
curl_setopt($client, CURLOPT_RETURNTRANSFER, 1);
$response = curl_exec($client);
curl_close($client);

$xml = simplexml_load_string($response);

foreach ($xml->photos->photo as $photo) {
  $attributes = $photo->attributes();

  $image_url = 'http://farm' . $attributes['farm'] . '.static.flickr.
com/' . $attributes['server'] . '/' . $attributes['id'] . '_' .
$attributes['secret'] . '.jpg';
  echo '<img src=\'' . $image_url . '\'/>'."\n";

  $params = array (
    'method' => 'flickr.photos.getInfo',
    'api_key' => 'YOUR_API_KEY',
    'photo_id' => $attributes['id']
  );

  $query_string = '';
  foreach ($params as $key => $value) {
    $query_string .= "$key=" . urlencode($value) . "&";
  }

  $url = "$base_url?$query_string";

  $client = curl_init($url);
  curl_setopt($client, CURLOPT_RETURNTRANSFER, 1);
  $response = curl_exec($client);
  curl_close($client);

  $xml = simplexml_load_string($response);

  echo '<a href=\'' . $xml->photo->urls[0]->url . '\'>'. $xml->photo-
>title . '</a>' ."\n";

  echo "<ul>\n";
  foreach ($xml->photo->tags->tag as $tag)
    echo '<li>'. $tag . '</li>'."\n";
  echo "</ul>\n";
}
?>
```

In this sample, we first get 10 search results for the term `flowers`, and then for each photo in the search result `getInfo` operation is invoked in the Flickr REST API. The `getInfo` operation would return a response that looks like the following response:

```
<?xml version="1.0" encoding="utf-8" ?>
<rsp stat="ok">
<photo id="2426991275" secret="0880bd8ed7" server="2225" farm="3"
dateuploaded="1208690404" isfavorite="0" license="0" rotation="0" orig
inalsecret="eb3e38e1ee" originalformat="jpg" media="photo">
  <owner nsid="22966172@N03" username="joergschickedanz"
realname="Joerg Schickedanz" location="Leipzig, Germany" />
  <title>Im Garten April 2008</title>
  <description />
  <visibility ispublic="1" isfriend="0" isfamily="0" />
  <dates posted="1208690404" taken="2008-04-21 10:30:39"
takengranularity="0" lastupdate="1208690407" />
  <editability cancomment="0" canaddmeta="0" />
  <usage candownload="1" canblog="0" canprint="0" />
  <comments>0</comments>
  <notes />
  <tags>
    <tag id="22943118-2426991275-2620" author="22966172@N03"
raw="spring" machine_tag="0">spring</tag>
    <tag id="22943118-2426991275-236" author="22966172@N03"
raw="roses" machine_tag="0">roses</tag>
    <tag id="22943118-2426991275-140" author="22966172@N03"
raw="flowers" machine_tag="0">flowers</tag>
  </tags>
  <urls>
    <url type="photopage">http://www.flickr.com/photos/22966172@
N03/2426991275/</url>
  </urls>
</photo>
</rsp>
```

In our example PHP script, we extract the URL, title and the tags from this information. Note that the URL is not the URL of the image; rather it is the URL of the page in which Flickr displays the image.

The output of this script would be:

```
<img src='http://farm3.static.flickr.com/2374/2427821192_72c38a272e.
jpg'/>
<a href='http://www.flickr.com/photos/chrisilstrup/2427821192/
'>Crocus</a>
<ul>
<li>spring</li>
<li>flowers</li>
```

```
</ul>
<img src='http://farm3.static.flickr.com/2045/2427822144_f8157e450a.
jpg'/>
<a href='http://www.flickr.com/photos/mmakri/2427822144/'>Flower
Drops</a>
<ul>
<li>flower</li>
<li>drop</li>
<li>drops</li>
<li>water</li>
<li>flowers</li>
</ul>
```

Here is a sample screen shot from this script:

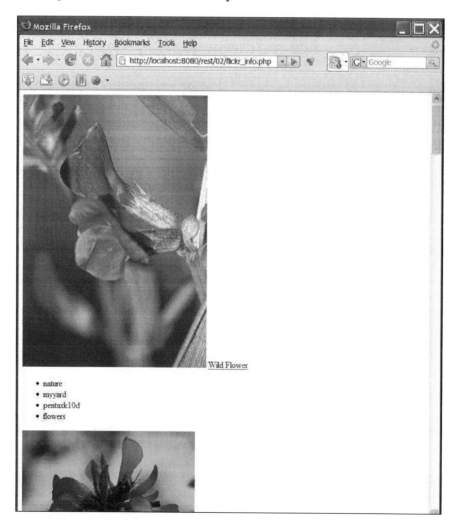

The PHP script does the job, but it is not the cleanest of the source code. There is considerable code duplication. It could be improved to make it more modular and also make the code more reusable for future REST applications that you would implement. Here is the same script, but with less code duplication and more modularity.

```php
<?php
function build_query_string(array $params) {
  $query_string = http_build_query($params);
  return $query_string;
}

function curl_get($url) {
  $client = curl_init($url);
  curl_setopt($client, CURLOPT_RETURNTRANSFER, true);
  $response = curl_exec($client);
  curl_close($client);
  return $response;
}

$base_url = 'http://api.flickr.com/services/rest/';
$api_key = 'YOUR_API_KEY';

$params = array (
  'method' => 'flickr.photos.search',
  'api_key' => $api_key,
  'tags' => 'flowers',
  'per_page' => 10
);

$url = "$base_url?" . build_query_string($params);

$response = curl_get($url);

$xml = simplexml_load_string($response);

foreach ($xml->photos->photo as $photo) {
  $attributes = $photo->attributes();

  $image_url = 'http://farm' . $attributes['farm'] . '.static.flickr.
com/' . $attributes['server'] . '/' . $attributes['id'] . '_' .
$attributes['secret'] . '.jpg';
  echo '<img src=\'' . $image_url . '\'/>' . "\n";

  $params = array (
    'method' => 'flickr.photos.getInfo',
    'api_key' => $api_key,
    'photo_id' => $attributes['id']
  );

  $url = "$base_url?" . build_query_string($params);

  $response = curl_get($url);
```

```php
$xml = simplexml_load_string($response);
echo '<a href=\'' . $xml->photo->urls[0]->url . '\'>' . $xml->photo-
>title . '</a>' . "\n";
echo "<ul>\n";
foreach ($xml->photo->tags->tag as $tag)
  echo '<li>' . $tag . '</li>' . "\n";
echo "</ul>\n";
}
?>
```

The output from the script is as follows:

So many roses, so little time...

- pink
- red
- rose
- fleur
- flower
- flowers
- fleurs
- france

In this section, it was demonstrated how to use CURL HTTP client library and SimpleXML parser API to consume Flickr REST API. If you are interested in a complete PHP library that can be used to make use of more operations, `http://sourceforge.net/projects/phlickr/` would be a good choice.

Summary

While providing and consuming REST style web services, the primary pre-requisites are an HTTP server or an HTTP client library and an XML parser library. In this chapter, we saw how to use the PHP CURL API to consume web services using various HTTP verbs such as HTTP GET, POST, PUT and DELETE. The DOM API and SimpleXML API for building XML object structures and parsing XML streams were also discussed.

We discussed in detail how to build XML request payloads and also how to parse XML response payloads.

The final section of this chapter demonstrated how to use the HTTP client features and XML parser features to invoke the Flickr REST API.

phpFlickr (http://sourceforge.net/projects/phpflickr) provides a PHP class that wraps the Flickr API. It has easy to use functions and also contains functions that aggregate data from multiple Flickr API methods. PEAR::Flickr_API (http://code.iamcal.com/php/flickr/readme.htm) is another PHP package that provides an easy to use PHP class to deal with the Flickr API. Apart from using them to consume Flickr services, you can also use them to understand REST programming principles by having a look into the source code of these packages.

In the next chapter, we will look into some example use cases where REST is used in the real world.

3
REST in the Real World

There is a wide use of REST style services today. Many web applications provide REST style interfaces so that the developers can implement value added applications using the REST interfaces of those web applications.

In this chapter, we are going to use some of those publicly available REST style services and build our own value added content. Some of the services that we will be using are:

- BBC news feeds
- Yahoo news search
- Yahoo maps
- Yahoo local search
- Earthquakes feed

Types of Services Available

The REST style services available today have many forms. Some have custom APIs defined, where we can find API documents defining the input, output formats, and the resource URI information. Examples are the Flickr API, Amazon API, and Yahoo REST API.

There are various XML feeds such as RSS feeds and Atom Feeds available around the Web today. As an example, news websites and Weblogs (better known as Blogs) use either RSS or Atom feeds to reflect the latest updates. Since they also deal with information we can also consider those as a form of REST style services. Feeds provide users with frequently updated content and hence are often used for distributing news. There are two main feed formats, RSS (http://en.wikipedia.org/wiki/RSS_(file_format)) and ATOM (http://en.wikipedia.org/wiki/Atom_(standard)). All major news sites as well as blogs have associated feeds in both formats.

Some of the REST style services can also deliver formats other than XML. The simplest example is the use of images while using a map related applications such as Google Maps or Yahoo Maps. The JSON (http://www.json.org/) standard is also popular. PHP allows for different input/output formats to be dealt with flexibly. One of the advantages of REST is its diversity and adaptability to make use of the flexibility that PHP provides. However, the basic REST principles do not change irrespective of the opportunity to use various message formats.

Consuming Real-World Services

In this section, we will explore how to consume REST services and build value added applications on top of those services.

Before consuming a service, understanding the service involves several steps:

- Find out what the input parameters and format of those parameters are and prepare the input
- Find out the service endpoint that is the URL, and the HTTP verb expected. Some services also expect particular content type information
- Find out the response format and explore how to process the expected response to pick the information required out of the response
- Check the terms of use of the service:
    - API rate limits
      Depending on API rate limits, that is how much does it cost to invoke a single operation using the API, our approach might differ with intermediate proxying or other variants of preserving/caching results of API calls.
    - Copyright implications
      Some of the content that you receive as a result of an API call might be copyrighted. You have to be sensitive to copyright implications before using that content in your web application.
    - Service level commitments
      While using a publicly available service, there could be situations that the service provider is strained due to too many people accessing the service concurrently. So the service provider would define some service level constraints in terms of quality of the service. As an example, if you have performance commitments in your web application, then you have to be sensitive to response time commitments from the service. If you want to display the results from the service on your web application within an acceptable time period,

where your web application's users would not feel it to be too slow, you may have to be sensitive to response time service level constraints defined by the service provider.

Note that most API documents explicitly mention if a given input parameter is mandatory or optional. You must pay attention to those details to ensure that all mandatory parameters are present in a request. Similarly, the output from the service could also have mandatory as well as optional parts. While you can assume the mandatory parts to be present, your response processing logic must have provisions to deal with optional parts, or else your application may fail.

Interpreting APIs could get complicated based on the way the API is designed. While using REST services designed and deployed by others, we often have no control over the way it is designed and we cannot afford to change it ourselves. Hence the chances are that we need to learn how to live with those public REST service APIs that we want to use.

If you have difficulties understanding the service API documents, try to send a request to the service, capture the response and print it out. Most API documents provide dummy request/response as templates. You can use those to help you build the request for your initial tests. If the API documents do not provide those, you could try to create dummy request/responses templates based on whatever information is provided in the API documentation. These steps help you build confidence on the service API in the prototyping phase. Also note that most services often provide us with a sandbox to help developers play around with the API and get familiar with the API.

During the prototyping phase, the chances are that you will run into errors. Pay attention to the error information returned in the error messages. Often, the error information could lead you to clues as to how you could solve the problems.

Once you have some basic understanding and get your first few requests to work then you can read the API document carefully to find more details.

It should also be mentioned that service APIs often change because the services evolve over time and your client code should be able to deal with the changing mandatory/required fields. Thus, creating abstraction layers is always a good idea to deal with the API changes. Also, while interpreting APIs, it's good to never rely on personal findings. Sometimes, looking at a particular response to a request, you may come up with some assumptions on the format for the response. Make sure you try several different request scenarios with several different valid and invalid values for input parameters before you make such assumptions. Make things as robust as possible so that your XML parser can deal with position-changes of XML elements and maybe not even use XML strict parsing.

Cresting our Utility Code—RESTUtil.php

Let's define some utility functions that we are going to use for the samples throughout this chapter.

This would help us to modularize our client PHP scripts and make sure that we re-use the utility functions. It will lead us to focus more on the business logic while implementing client scripts without having to worry about the repetitive tasks such as building the query strings and forming the CURL options for HTTP GET requests. Please note that we can use REST services without this utility script, but this script would help us to be more organized while implementing client scripts.

We will name this script RESTUtil.php.

```php
<?php
function build_query_string(array $params) {
    $query_string = http_build_query($params);
    return $query_string;
}
function curl_get($url) {
    $client = curl_init($url);
    curl_setopt($client, CURLOPT_RETURNTRANSFER, true);
    $response = curl_exec($client);
    curl_close($client);
    return $response;
}
?>
```

The build_query_string function builds the HTTP query string for a given request parameter array.

The curl_get function would execute a GET request on the given URL and return the response. Note that this function assumes that the given URL would include the query parameters, if any, required by the service.

Consuming an RSS Feed—BBC News Feed

The BBC provides a number of news feeds on various categories of news. You can find the feed URLs at http://news.bbc.co.uk/2/hi/help/3223484.stm.

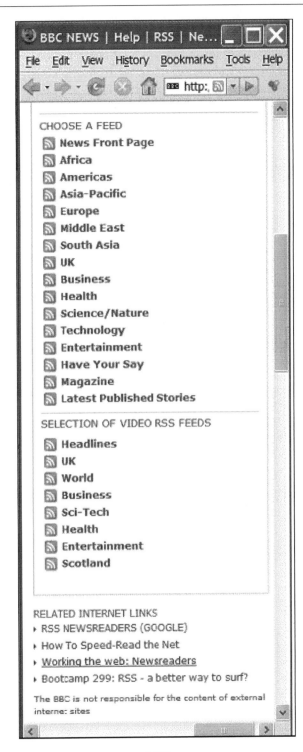

In the next PHP script we will access the technology news feed.

```php
<?php
require_once 'RESTUtil.php';

$url = 'http://newsrss.bbc.co.uk/rss/newsonline_world_edition/
technology/rss.xml';

$response = curl_get($url);

$xml = simplexml_load_string($response);

foreach ($xml->channel->item as $item) {
    echo $item->title . "\n";
}
?>
```

First of all, note that we include the `RESTUtil.php` with utility functions at the top of the source code. The output generated when the PHP script is run is shown below:

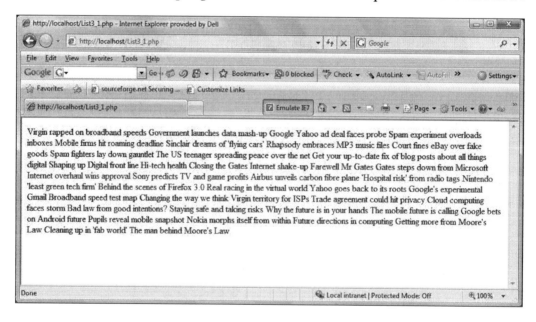

The response from the feed would be in RSS version 2.0 format. You can find more information on RSS formats form `http://www.rssboard.org/rss-history`. The following XML snippet shows the format of the response received. Note that the following XML is what you receive from the service located at `http://newsrss.bbc.co.uk/rss/newsonline_world_edition/technology/rss.xml`. The client PHP script that was shown above process this XML response in order to prepare its output, which is shown above.

```
<?xml version="1.0" encoding="ISO-8859-1" ?>
<?xml-stylesheet title="XSL_formatting" type="text/xsl" href="/shared/
bsp/xsl/rss/nolsol.xsl"?>
<rss version="2.0" xmlns:media="http://search.yahoo.com/mrss">
    <channel>
        <item>
            <title>Future web</title>
            <description>
                Luminaries predict the shape of tomorrow's world wide
                web
            </description>
            <link>
                http://news.bbc.co.uk/go/rss/
                                    -/2/hi/technology/7373717.stm
            </link>
            <guid isPermaLink="false">
                http://news.bbc.co.uk/1/hi/technology/7373717.stm
            </guid>
            <pubDate>Wed, 30 Apr 2008 09:32:41 GMT</pubDate>
            <category>Technology</category>
        </item>
        <item>
            <title>The offline cost of an online life</title>
            <description>
                Bill Thompson wonders if his virtual presences are
                having a significant real world impact.
            </description>
            <link>
                http://news.bbc.co.uk/go/rss/
                                    -/2/hi/technology/7300403.stm
            </link>
            <guid isPermaLink="false">
                http://news.bbc.co.uk/1/hi/technology/7300403.stm
            </guid>
            <pubDate>Tue, 18 Mar 2008 08:53:18 GMT</pubDate>
            <category>Technology</category>
        </item>
    </channel>
</rss>
```

There are multiple item elements in the response representing Technology news elements. In the PHP source code from the XML tree, we print out the title of each news item. Based on the requirements of your program, you can choose to pick any of the other sub-elements from each `item` element. As an example, if you want the news link you could have used:

```php
echo $item->link . "\n";
```

Printing out the feed is very straightforward. Let's see how to combine the information from the feed with another Service.

BBC News Feed with Yahoo News Search

In this example, we would pick the titles from the BBC news feed and search for the related news items for Yahoo news search.

```php
<?php
require_once 'RESTUtil.php';

$url = 'http://newsrss.bbc.co.uk/rss/newsonline_world_edition/
technology/
 rss.xml';

$response = curl_get($url);

$xml = simplexml_load_string($response);

$base_url = 'http://search.yahooapis.com/NewsSearchService/V1/
newsSearch';

foreach ($xml->channel->item as $item) {
    echo '<h2>' . $item->title . '</h2>'. "\n";

    $params = array (
        'appid' => 'YahooDemo',
        'query' => $item->title,
        'results' => 2,
        'language' => 'en'
    );

    $url = "$base_url?" . build_query_string($params);

    $response = curl_get($url);
    $xml = simplexml_load_string($response);

    echo '<ul>' ."\n";
    foreach ($xml->Result as $news) {
        echo '<li><a href=\'' . $news->Url . '\'/>' . $news->Title . '</
a></li>' . "\n";
    }
    echo '</ul>' ."\n";
}
?>
```

This source code is self-descriptive.

Here is the logical breakdown of the script:

- Fetch the news feed.
- First we define the feed URL.

  ```
  $url = 'http://newsrss.bbc.co.uk/rss/newsonline_world_edition/
  technology/rss.xml';
  ```

- Then we get the feed content using CURL and capture the response.

  ```
  $response = curl_get($url);
  ```

- Next we build the SimpleXML object structure using the received response.

  ```
  $xml = simplexml_load_string($response);
  ```

- For each news title, search Yahoo for related news.
- Using the XML object structure that we build based on the response, we can find out the news title of each news item.

  ```
  foreach ($xml->channel->item as $item) {
      echo '<h2>' . $item->title . '</h2>'. "\n";
  ```

Then for each news `item` title, while staying in the for loop, we prepare the array of parameters to be used with Yahoo search query.

```
$params = array (
    'appid' => 'YahooDemo',
    'query' => $item->title,
    'results' => 2,
    'language' => 'en'
);
```

- Note that we are going to search for the news `item`'s title, and we are looking for two search results, as well as our language preference is English.
- And next, we build the query string using the array of parameters.

  ```
  $url = "$base_url?" . build_query_string($params);
  ```

- Note that our base URL is:

  ```
  $base_url = 'http://search.yahooapis.com/NewsSearchService/V1/
  newsSearch';
  ```

- This is the URL where Yahoo News Search is located.

- Next, we send a GET request to the URL using CURL, capture the response, and build a SimpleXML object structure using the response.

```
$response = curl_get($url);
$xml = simplexml_load_string($response);
```

- Now we are ready to use the news results from Yahoo and display them in a useful format.

- Print out the result picking the required data elements and formatting them to suit the desired output.

- For each news result item in the XML structure that we built using the response, we pick the news URL and link that with the news title.

```
foreach ($xml->Result as $news) {
    echo '<li><a href=\'' . $news->Url . '\'/>' . $news->Title .
    '</a></li>' . "\n";
```

- Here is a fragment of the output from this program.

```
<h2>The offline cost of an online life</h2>
<ul>
<li><a href='http://www.ecommercetimes.com/rsstory/62852.html'/
>eBay, Craigslist Soap Opera Unfolds</a></li>
<li><a href='http://www.onrec.com/newsstories/21420.asp'/>Issue
102 - 5th April - 1st May</a></li>
</ul>
<h2>Future web</h2>
<ul>
<li><a href='http://www.cnn.com/2008/SHOWBIZ/TV/05/01/tv.future/
index.html?section=cnn_latest'/>Is the future of TV on the Web?</a></
li>
<li><a href='http://news.bbc.co.uk/go/rss/-/1/hi/
technology/7373717.stm'/>Luminaries look to the future web</a></li>
</ul>
```

The output looks very interesting:

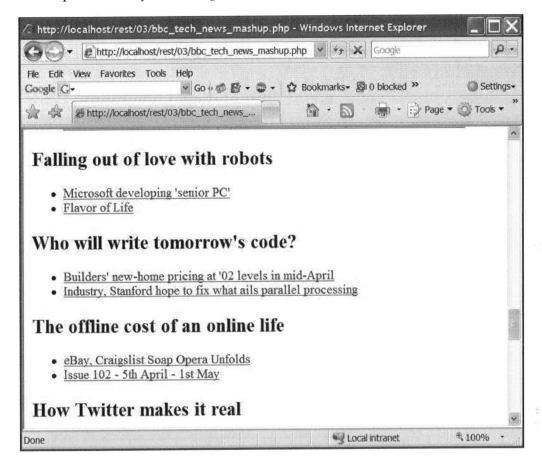

Yahoo Maps and Local Search

Yahoo maps and Google Maps are popular map serving applications on today's Internet. Both these applications provide us with REST APIs, so we can build interesting map related applications.

In this section, we will see how to combine the results of a local search and show the results on a map. Yahoo provides an AJAX based API to fetch a map and display it on a web browser. The API documentation is found at `http://developer.yahoo.com/maps/ajax/index.html`. Yahoo also provides a local search API, using which one can search for businesses near a specified location. The API for this service can be found at `http://developer.yahoo.com/search/local/V3/localSearch.html`. In the next PHP sample source code, we will use the local API to search hotels near Cambridge, MA area, and display them on a map.

Please note that in order to use the Yahoo! maps services, you need to get an application developer ID by registering at `https://developer.yahoo.com/wsregapp/`.

In the following sample, we are using a mix of JavaScript and PHP. One could have done all the processing with AJAX and not use PHP at all. One of the advantages of using PHP is that it is a feature rich language compared to JavaScript. Hence, if you have to do some complex processing, you would be better-off doing them with PHP on server side before pushing the results to the web browser. Note that AJAX processing happens within the web browser on the user machine, whereas PHP processing happens on server side.

If everything is done in PHP, there is a chance that the user would notice a delay in response because all processing happens before anything is sent to be displayed on the web browser. If everything is done on the web browser using AJAX, the user experience again can be affected by the resources available on the user machine. So there needs to be a correct mix of JavaScript and PHP used, and the correct mix needs to be figured out through experimenting based on the kind of application that you are building.

One of the other key aspects that must be kept in mind while using AJAX is the Web browser compatibility issues. Different Web browsers like Firefox and Internet Explorer can behave differently for the same piece of JavaScript code. If you stick to PHP and HTML alone, these could be avoided, however, JavaScript comes in handy when developing web applications with rich user experience.

```php
<?php
require_once 'RESTUtil.php';

function location_search($query, $in_location) {
    $base_url = 'http://local.yahooapis.com/LocalSearchService/V3/localSearch';

    $params = array (
        'appid' => 'YahooDemo',
        'query' => $query,
        'location' => $in_location
    );
    $url = $base_url . "?" . build_query_string($params);
    $response = curl_get($url);

    $xml = simplexml_load_string($response);
    foreach ($xml->Result as $location) {
      $data = array((string)$location->Latitude, (string)$location->Longitude,
          (string)$location->Title);
      $output[] = $data;
```

```php
        }
        return $output;
    }

function write_map_script(array $points) {
    // center map on the middle result and draw
    if (count($points) > 0) {
        $middle_point = $points[count($points) / 2];
        $js_middle = <<<JAVA_SCRIPT
            var points = new YGeoPoint($middle_point[0], $middle_
point[1]);
            map.drawZoomAndCenter(points, 5);
JAVA_SCRIPT;
        foreach ($points as $id => $obj) {
            $map_point_name = addslashes($obj[2]);
            $js_end = <<<JAVA_SCRIPT
                var point$id =
                new YGeoPoint($obj[0],$obj[1]);
                var current_marker = new YMarker(point$id);
                current_marker.addLabel('$id');
                current_marker.addAutoExpand('<div class="mp">$map_
point_name</div>');
                map.addOverlay(current_marker);
JAVA_SCRIPT;
        $js_middle .= $js_end;
        }
    }
    echo $js_middle . $js_end;
}

$points = location_search('Hotel', 'Cambridge, MA');

?>

<html>
  <head>
    <script type="text/javascript" src="http://api.maps.yahoo.com/aja
xymap?v=3.0&appid=1d023cfa8f244bbacc42b7d67658ba3d">
    </script>
    <style>
      #mapHolder {
        height: 700px;
        width: 700px;
      }
    </style>
```

```
  </head>
  <body>
    <div id="mapHolder"></div>
    <script type="text/javascript">
      var map = new YMap(document.getElementById('mapHolder'), YAHOO_
MAP_REG);
      map.addZoomShort();
      map.addPanControl();
      <?php write_map_script($points); ?>

    </script>
  </body>
</html>
```

Though this source code is a bit lengthier, we can easily break this down into several logical sections.

- Function implementations
- Calling functions to do the search and update the map
- HTML display

We have two functions in this source code. One is `location_search()` and the other is `write_map_script()`.

```
function location_search($query, $in_location) {
```

The `location_search()` function does search for given businesses in a given location. The first parameter to this function indicates the kind of business to search for and the second parameter indicates the area to search. In this example, the value of the first parameter is `Hotel` and the second parameter is `Cambridge, MA`, because we want to search for hotels around the Cambridge area.

The code within the `location_search()` function should be very familiar to you by now. We build the URL using the base URL and the query parameters string.

```
    $base_url = 'http://local.yahooapis.com/LocalSearchService/V3/
localSearch';

    $params = array (
        'appid' => 'YahooDemo',
        'query' => $query,
        'location' => $in_location
    );
    $url = $base_url . "?" . build_query_string($params);
```

Send the request using CURL API.

```
$response = curl_get($url);
```

Receive the response and process the response XML to pick the information we want.

```
$xml = simplexml_load_string($response);
foreach ($xml->Result as $location) {
    $data = array((string)$location->Latitude, (string)$location-
>Longitude,
        (string)$location->Title);
    $output[] = $data;
}
```

In this case, for each search result item, we are picking up the latitude, longitude and the title. Latitude and longitude are required to mark the point on the map and the title would be used to display the tip when the user moves the mouse over the marked point on the map.

The second function is `write_map_script()` and is used to build the JavaScript required to mark the points on the map with the search results. We use the `YMap` and `YGeoPoint` classes from the Yahoo AJAX map API.

To understand the flow of this source code, you have to start reading the code from the line:

```
$points = location_search('Hotel', 'Cambridge, MA');
```

This line is the entry point to the code, from here you can move to `location_search()` function and follow the code located there and come back to the above line and follow the code down to the HTML section.

Note that, while using PHP and JavaScript, you may come up with situations where you have to interchange data between PHP and JavaScript. Passing values of PHP variables to JavaScript is demonstrated in the following sample. You can use a PHP string and build the JavaScript code and at the same time use PHP variables.

```
$js_middle = <<<JAVA_SCRIPT
    var points = new YGeoPoint($middle_point[0], $middle_
point[1]);
        map.drawZoomAndCenter(points, 5);
JAVA_SCRIPT;
```

The other interesting question is if we can pass variable values in JavaScript to PHP. One way of accomplishing this is to generate JavaScript code with PHP, and have the browser refresh itself, passing specific variables back to the PHP script. See `http://php.net/manual/en/faq.html.php#faq.html.javascript-variable` for more details. Another option is to use XMLHttpRequest (`http://www.w3.org/TR/XMLHttpRequest/`) and make a call to the PHP script.

In the HTML section, we first import the Yahoo AJAX map script:

```
<script type="text/javascript" src="http://api.maps.yahoo.com/ajaxy
map?v=3.0&appid=your_api_key">
</script>
```

Note that you must replace `your_api_key` with your Yahoo API key for this sample to work for you.

Within the HTML section we have a PHP code snippet where we call the `write_map_script()` with the points array returned by the `location_search()` function. And the `write_map_script()` would do what is necessary to mark the points on the map corresponding to the search results.

Here is the output from this script.

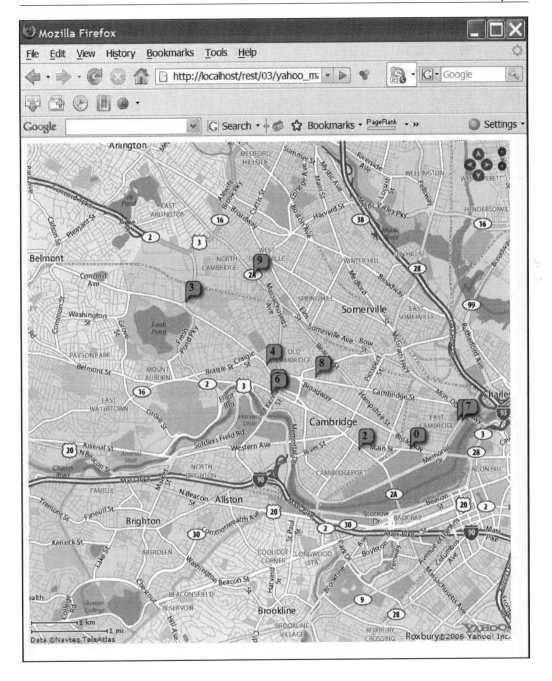

One of the interesting things to note with Yahoo local search API is that it is capable of giving you the output in both JSON as well as PHP serialized format in addition to the XML format that we used in the above example. In case you want to use the PHP serialization format for output, you need to set the output parameter to the value php, and need to use the unserialize function (http://www.php.net/manual/en/function.unserialize.php) to convert the received response to a PHP array.

Here is the same example, with PHP output format used for local search.

```php
<?php
require_once 'RESTUtil.php';

function location_search($query, $in_location) {
    $base_url = 'http://local.yahooapis.com/LocalSearchService/V3/
localSearch';

    $params = array (
        'appid' => 'YahooDemo',
        'output' => 'php',
        'query' => $query,
        'location' => $in_location
    );
    $url = $base_url . "?" . build_query_string($params);
    $response = curl_get($url);

    $output = unserialize($response);
    return $output['ResultSet']['Result'];
}

function write_map_script(array $points) {
    // center map on the middle result and draw
    if (count($points) > 0) {
        $middle_point = $points[count($points) / 2];
        $js_middle = <<<JAVA_SCRIPT
            var points = new YGeoPoint($middle_point[0], $middle_
point[1]);
            map.drawZoomAndCenter(points, 5);
JAVA_SCRIPT;
        foreach ($points as $id => $obj) {
            $map_point_name = addslashes($obj[2]);
            $js_end = <<<JAVA_SCRIPT
                var point$id =
                new YGeoPoint($obj[0],$obj[1]);
                var current_marker = new YMarker(point$id);
            current_marker.addLabel('$id');
            current_marker.addAutoExpand(
'<div class="mp">$map_point_name</div>');
```

```
                 map.addOverlay(current_marker);
JAVA_SCRIPT;
            $js_middle .= $js_end;
            }
        }
        echo $js_middle . $js_end;
}

$results = location_search('Hotel', ' Cambridge, MA');

foreach ($results as $id => $data) {
    $points[$id] = array (
        $data['Latitude'],
        $data['Longitude'],
        $data['Title']
    );
}
?>

<html>
  <head>
    <script type="text/javascript" src="http://api.maps.yahoo.com/ajaxy
map?v=3.0&appid=your_api_key">
    </script>
     <style>
       #mapHolder {
         height: 700px;
         width: 700px;
       }
     </style>
  </head>
  <body>
    <div id="mapHolder"></div>
    <script type="text/javascript">
        var map = new YMap(document.getElementById('mapHolder'),
YAHOO_MAP_REG);
        map.addZoomShort();
        map.addPanControl();
    <?php write_map_script($points); ?>
    </script>
  </body>
</html>
```

Note that, not only has the `location_search()` function been slightly changed, but the way that the return value from that function is being processed. In the previous version of this sample we picked the XML elements that we wanted and prepared the points array. However, in this sample, we are processing the array returned as a serialized PHP object and we pick the array elements that we want from that array and build the points array. While using the XML format, the application is easier to debug because the messages passed back and forth between the service and our script would be human readable. However, while using the serialized PHP format, it would be harder to debug the script as the messages sent are in binary format and are not readable.

The advantage of using binary serialized PHP format is that it is more efficient compared to the XML format. On one hand, the serialized PHP format would be compact compared to the XML message format. Apart from the real valuable content, an XML message needs XML element name tags to mark the boundaries between element contents and that makes the XML message bulky. The other fact to note is that, while using XML format, there needs to be some XML processing to extract the required data form the incoming XML message. However, while using serialized PHP objects, we just need to call the `unserialize()` method. This is far more efficient than parsing and processing the XML message.

Earthquakes and Yahoo Maps

In the previous sample we used a Yahoo service that gave us latitude and longitude directly. However, there could be situations where we have to find or compute those values. `http://www.ga.gov.au/rss/quakesfeed.rss` gives an RSS feed of the earthquakes that have taken place. The longitude and latitude information is embedded in the `description` tag within `item`.

```
<item>
    <title>04/05/2008 22:14:32(UTC) North East of Northam, WA
(Preliminary)</title>
    <link>http://www.ga.gov.au/bin/earthquake.pl?title=North+East+of+No
rtham%2C+WA+%28Preliminary%29&amp;magnitude=3.8&amp;depth=0&amp;xy=117
.580,-31.127&amp;date=04,05,2008&amp;time=22,14,32&amp;bg1=eqrisk_lm&a
mp;zoom=100&amp;station=MORW</link>
    <description> Latitude: -31.127 Longitude: 117.58 Magnitude: 3.8
Depth(km): 0</description>
</item>
```

We can pick the latitude and longitude information from the description tag's text using the `split()` operation. Then we can use logic similar to the Yahoo local search program. However, it is simpler to extract the longitude and latitude information using `xy` parameter in the `link` tag.

First we can locate the `link` element using the code snippet:

```
$item->link
```

This string would have the form:

```
http://www.ga.gov.au/bin/earthquake.pl?title=North+East+of+Northam%2
C+WA+%28Preliminary%29&amp;magnitude=3.8&amp;depth=0&amp;xy=117.580,
-31.127&amp;date=04,05,2008&amp;time=22,14,32&amp;bg1=eqrisk_lm&amp;zo
om=100&amp;station=MORW
```

To mark the map, we need to pick the latitude and longitude from this string. In the xy parameter, x maps to longitude and y maps to latitude.

We can use `parse_str` function to split the string and pick the `xy` parameter.

```
parse_str($item->link, $params);
```

Then we can split the `xy` parameter to pick the coordinates that map to the longitude and the latitude.

```
$coords = split(",", $params['xy']);
```

Here is the complete code for this example:

```php
<?php
require_once 'RESTUtil.php';

function get_quakes() {
    $url = 'http://www.ga.gov.au/rss/quakesfeed.rss';
    $response = curl_get($url);

    $xml = simplexml_load_string($response);
    foreach ($xml->channel->item as $item) {
      parse_str($item->link, $params);
      $coords = split(",", $params['xy']);
      $data = array($coords[1], $coords[0],
          (string)$item->title);;
      $output[] = $data;
    }
    return $output;

}

function write_map_script(array $points) {
    // center map on the middle result and draw
    if (count($points) > 0) {
        $middle_point = $points[count($points) / 2];
        $js_middle = <<<JAVA_SCRIPT
```

```php
            var points = new YGeoPoint($middle_point[0], $middle_
point[1]);
            map.drawZoomAndCenter(points, 16);
JAVA_SCRIPT;
        foreach ($points as $id => $obj) {
            $map_point_name = addslashes($obj[2]);
              $js_end = <<<JAVA_SCRIPT
                var point$id =
                new YGeoPoint($obj[0],$obj[1]);
                  var current_marker = new YMarker(point$id);
                current_marker.addLabel('$id');
                current_marker.addAutoExpand(
'<div class="mp">$map_point_name</div>');
                map.addOverlay(current_marker);
JAVA_SCRIPT;
            $js_middle .= $js_end;
            }
        }
    echo $js_middle . $js_end;
}
$points = get_quakes();
?>
<html>
  <head>
    <script type="text/javascript" src="http://api.maps.yahoo.com/ajaxy
map?v=3.0&appid=your_api_key">
    </script>
     <style>
       #mapHolder {
         height: 700px;
         width: 700px;
       }
     </style>
  </head>
  <body>
    <div id="mapHolder"></div>
    <script type="text/javascript">
        var map = new YMap(document.getElementById('mapHolder'),
YAHOO_MAP_REG);
        map.addZoomShort();
        map.addPanControl();
    <?php write_map_script($points); ?>
    </script>
  </body>
</html>
```

And the output would look like:

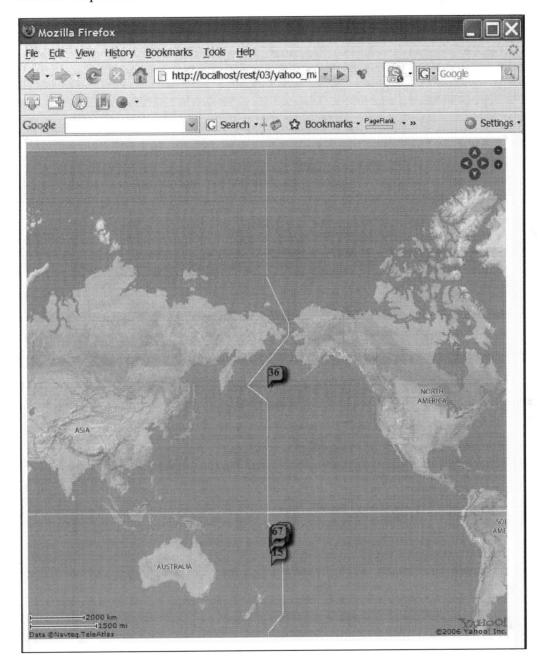

Mashups

A mashup is an application that combines multiple data sources into a single application. The rise of REST style applications available on the Internet enhanced the interest on Mahup applications as well.

Almost all examples that were given in this chapter could be considered mashup style applications. As an example, we combined the BBC news feeds with Yahoo news search to locate related news items.

Mashing up map data with other location related data is a very popular breed of applications today. The local search application and the earthquake application examples that we explored in this chapter fall into that category.

If you want to build mashups using the techniques that were introduced in this chapter, you can find information on publicly available information from programmableweb.com website. See http://www.programmableweb.com/apis/ directory/1?sort=mashups for more information. This website has a very nice categorization so that you can find the kind of web service that you are looking for with ease. As an example, if you want weather information services, go to the weather link on the left-hand side menu.

PHP Web 2.0 Mashup Projects: Practical PHP Mashups with Google Maps, Flickr, Amazon, YouTube, MSN Search, Yahoo! is a book on mashup technologies from PACKT Publishing. You can find more information on this book from http://www.packtpub.com/php-web-20-mashups/book.

Summary

In this chapter we looked into some of the real world applications and learned how to combine multiple service interfaces to build value added custom applications.

In previous chapters, we have seen how to access Flickr API. In this chapter, we saw how to use RSS or ATOM feeds, Yahoo search API, and Yahoo maps API.

With the know-how you gained so far in this book, you could build very powerful value added applications like mashups using publicly available REST style services. The concepts covered so far include:

- Using correct HTTP method to retrieve data from services
- Using XML parsers for building requests and parsing responses
- Consume XML feeds, example RSS or ATOM feeds

- Steps involved in understanding a service API, both technical and non-technical
- Best practices to be followed in the prototyping phase
- Abstracting out re-usable functionality into utility classes or libraries
- Combining multiple service iterations to build value-added applications
- Mixing up PHP and JavaScript
- Dealing with message formats other than XML such as serialized PHP
- Working with application specific details such as request/response formats and extracting the information we want from the response using PHP functionality
- A brief introduction to Mashups

In the next chapter, we will explore how to design a RESTful service from ground-up, this will help you to understand how to apply REST principles and design your own services. We will also implement the designed service using PHP from scratch.

4
Resource-Oriented Services

Resource Oriented Services are services that are designed in accordance with the REST architectural principles. As we discussed in the first chapter, the concept of a resource is at the heart of REST principles. Every service is a resource with a unique identifier. Hence the term "Resource Oriented".

In this chapter, we will study in detail and from ground-up how to design and implement services to comply with REST architectural principles. We will use a real world example, a simplified library system to learn from scratch how to design a system with REST principles in mind.

Designing Services

While designing services in compliance with REST architectural principles, the initial steps to be followed are not much different from those that would be followed architecting a software system with other techniques. First and foremost, the real world problem to be solved or the set of goals to be achieved with the system needs to be understood well. Often this is done through a **requirements specification**. The simplest requirements specification could be to define the problem in writing, using a natural language like English. May be a paragraph or two could be used to describe the problem.

Then the problem needs to be analysed and the problem can be understood by software architects. This is called **requirements analysis**. In the requirements analysis phase, we need to understand the data sets that exist within the systems and the business operations that are related to those data sets. Business operations in this context refer to the functions that implement the problem domain-specific logic. As an example, if we are to implement a library system, borrowing a book and returning a book are two business operations of the system. The business operations process the data sets to yield value added data or information. Therefore, during the requirements analysis phase, we would also have to analyse the databases that would be used for the system. If we are to use existing databases, we would have to analyse and understand where the data would come from that is the data endpoints. If the databases are not already available, then the analysis phase would lead us to the information on what databases are to be designed for the system.

Given a problem description, we can look for the **nouns** to identify data sets. In the REST architectural style, data sets or nouns in the problem description turns out to be the resources. The data sets are so fundamental in the system that they need to be properly evaluated. Common groupings are important to not create redundancy. It is also important to have a flexible foundation for the system so that there is room for expansion later on, as the system evolves.

Once the resources are identified, we need to do some designwork on those resources. First, the resources need to be named. This is quite straightforward. We used the nouns to identify resources and those nouns themselves could be used to name the resources. Once the resources are identified, we can identify those resources with common attributes and group them into collections of resources.

The next step is to map URIs to each and every business operation of the resources. We can use a table structure to tabulate the resource and business operations against the URIs.

Sometimes, the business operations require some algorithmic parameters. Query variables can be used for algorithmic resources and the names and possible value domains for query variables need to be identified. However, note that the use of query parameters to differentiate between resources and business operations are highly discouraged in REST architectural principle.

In addition to the URI mappings, the HTTP verbs are also important for business operations. A single resource URI could have multiple HTTP verbs associated depending on the semantics of the operations.

Now that we have had a look into the steps involved with the service design in a resource-oriented world, let's look into an example on how to design a resource-oriented system.

Simplified Library System

Here is a problem statement that describes the library system that we are going to use for the example:

"The library contains a wide array of books. It may have several copies of a given book. Any library member may borrow books for three weeks. Members of the library can borrow up to two books at a time. New books arrive regularly. The system must keep track of when books are borrowed and returned by members."

This is a very simplified description of a library system. However, this is a good enough problem for us to explore resource-oriented service principles.

Resource Design

As mentioned earlier, we can look for nouns in the problem description in search of resources. If you read the problem statement given earlier, there are two nouns that stand out.

- Book
- Member

So, books and members are the two primary resource collections in the library system.

Next, what are the main business operations in this system? If we consider a book, the key business operations are:

- Add new book
- List books
- Retrieve book
- Update book
- Remove book

We can map these operations to HTTP methods and URI combinations, as shown in the following table.

HTTP Method	URI	Description
GET	/book	List books
POST	/book	Create book(s)
GET	/book/1	Retrieve book
PUT	/book/1	Update book
DELETE	/book/1	Remove book

All of the above listed operations are related to the resource book. The first two operations operate on the resource collection. The last three operations in this example operate on a particular resource, the book ID **1**. The ID in the URL is not really a parameter, rather the whole URL, including the ID uniquely identify the particular resource, the book with ID 1.

Note that we have used the URL prefix /book and not /books as the prefix for resource locations related to book resource. This is because we deal with a single resource instance in most of the cases when it comes to operations. As an example, we would update the book with the ID 1, and the URL would read /book/1, and this naturally reads as "update the book with ID 1". If we had used /books/1, it would have to be read, "from books, update the book with ID 1". Since we want to use the same prefix for all the operations related to the book resource, even for listing books we use a /book. We could have used /books only for operation, however, then we would lose the conceptual grouping of operations related to book resource, because some operations would use a different URL format.

It is also important to note that one must use the correct HTTP verb to match the semantics of each operation.

PUT vs POST

At a higher level, we can think that anything that creates a new resource is a PUT operation and anything that changes an existing resource is a POST operation. However, according to the HTTP RFC 2616 (http://www.w3.org/Protocols/rfc2616/rfc2616.html), PUT puts a page at a specific URL. If there's already a page there, it's replaced. If there is no page there, a new one is created. As an example, if a PUT request is sent to /book/1, then it would check to see if that is already available and act accordingly. If one needs to update the book with ID 2, then /book/2 must be used. While sending a PUT request, you need to be more specific on the resource identification. Even though, in theory, it is possible to send a PUT request to a generic URL like /book, where you indicate that every book needs to be updated, in practice it becomes a complicated operation. Moreover, you would want to prevent such uses, because a user by mistake could delete all the books from the system, if such an operation was possible, even with proper security authentication and authorization mechanisms in place

POST sends some data to a specified URL and as per the HTTP specification. The server can do whatever it wants with this POST data. It can store it somewhere privately, it can store it in the page at the URL that was POSTed to, it can store it in a new page, it can use it as input for several different existing and new pages, or it can throw the information away.

In the real world, POST is more often used than PUT. The main reason for this is the fact that the PUT operation would be disabled by the service provider, especially in a shared hosting environments, for security reasons. Hence, we can afford to use POST to create as well as to update resources, however in theory, it may look incorrect.

URI Design

For the library system that we are using as the example, we identified two key resources, **book** and **member**.

For operating on a particular book, we can use the book ID, the entity attribute that can be used to uniquely identify a resource instance. Likewise, we can use the member ID for members. We can append these attributes to the URI to help uniquely identify the resource instances.

```
Books       /book/{book_id}
Member      /member/{member_id}
```

The above two URI patterns can be used for operations related to the two key resources in our example problem domain. Combined with HTTP verbs, they can cater for the **CRUD (Create, Read, Update** and **Delete)** operations for the resources.

There are some operations that are a bit more complex than the style of operations described above that involve more than a single resource. As an example, consider a member borrowing a book. There are two resources involved in that operation, a member and a book, so does the return book operation. The borrow and return operations need to identify both the member and the book involved uniquely. The following URI patterns cater for those requirements.

```
Borrow      /member/{member_id}/books/{book_id}
Return      /member/{member_id}/books/{book_id}
```

To indicate that the member with ID 10 wants to borrow the book with ID 3, we can use:

```
/member/10/books/3
```

Similarly, if the same member borrows book the book with ID 7, we can use:

```
/member/10/books/7
```

For borrow and return operations, member is the primary resource. A member can borrow up to two books as per the problem statement, hence there can be more than one book associated with a member at a given time. Book is the secondary resource in these operations. Therefore the member appears first in the URI and the book appears second.

If you consider the data storage in a database for the borrow and return operations, it would use a combined primary key, consisting of the member ID and the book ID. However, while mapping these data to the resources in the REST style application, we would have to represent this information using a resource with a unique URI. In that case, we need to decide what appears first and what appears second in the URI.

If we are to interchange the ordering of where the member and book identifiers appear in the URI, then it would lead to ambiguities. Hence it would be a good practice to identify a primary resource. In the real world, a member would pick up a book from the shelf and walk to the counter to borrow it, or bring a borrowed book to the counter to return it. Hence we can say that it is the member who initiates the operations such as `borrow` and `return` of the books, and because of that we have chosen to make sure that member identifier appears first in the URI. When there are multiple resources involved with an operation, you could choose any ordering in the URI design to include them in the resource identifier. However, it always makes understanding and maintaining the system easier if we consider the real world scenarios while choosing the URI ordering.

Another important point to note on the design of the URI mapping is that we did not use the operation name in the URI. As an example, we could have used `/borrow/member/X/books/Y/` or `/return/member/X/books/Y/`. While using REST, we operate on resources and the HTTP verbs we use to indicate the nature of the operation. Therefore, to understand the operations you have to consider both the URI as well as the HTTP verb used on that URI. The next section describes this URI and HTTP verb mapping.

URI and HTTP Verb Mapping

The final step of the resource-oriented service design is to come up with the mapping between URI and HTTP verb mapping for the business operations. The following table contains the mappings for the library system.

URI	HTTP Method	Collection	Operation	Business Operation
/book	GET	books	retrieve	Get books
/book	POST	books	create	Add book(s)
/book/{book_id}	GET	books	retrieve	Get book data
/member	GET	members	retrieve	Get members
/member	POST	members	create	Add member(s)
/member/{member_id}	GET	members	retrieve	Get member data
/member/{member_id}/ books	GET	members	retrieve	Get member borrowings
/member/{member_id}/ books/{book_id}	POST	members	create	Borrow book
/member/{member_id}/ books/{book_id}	DELETE	members	delete	Return book

For both book and member resources, we have `create` and `retrieve` operations. We also have a `retrieve` operation for a particular member or a book. To keep the system simple, we do not have a `delete` operation for book and member resources. So the assumption is, once a book or a member is added to the system, the record stays there forever.

For a given member, we can retrieve the member borrowings, providing the member ID with HTTP GET verb.

We also have the `borrow book` and `return book` business operations designed. Using POST verb, with member ID and book ID in the URI, we have the `borrow` operation and the same URI with DELETE verb would represent the `return` operation.

System Implementation

Now that we have the initial RESTful design of the library system in place, let's go ahead and implement the system using PHP. The first step is to create a database and for this we will be using some SQL statements. The next section explains the steps involved in creating the database.

Library Database

We would need persistent data storage for storing the library system's data. We could use a file or a database for this purpose. Let us use a simple MySQL database for this. As a reminder, you will be able to get scripts for creating the database from the code download. This is available on www.packtpub.com.

Activate the MySQL PHP extension in `php.ini` configuration file before using the MySQL database.

The design of the database tables is straightforward as we already have identified the resources. In our service design steps, that we followed so far, we have identified book and member to be our two main resources. These are going to be represented in our database entity model as well. Hence we will have two entities, in other words two database tables, named `book` and `member`.

Next, when we consider storing data related to the borrowing of books, we notice that a given member can borrow more than one book. Also, we can notice that a given book could be borrowed by more than one member over time. Hence the borrowing of a book would relate books and members in a **n:m** relationship, meaning **n** number of books could relate to **m** number of members. This is known as the relationship cardinality in the entity relationship modelling of databases. When the relationship cardinality is many to many, or **n:m**, then we require a separate table to represent that relationship. Hence we require a table named `borrowing` to represent books borrowed by the members.

Following are the SQL create statements for the database table design that we will use for the sample implementation.

```sql
CREATE TABLE 'book' (
   'id' int(11) NOT NULL auto_increment,
   'name' varchar(256) NOT NULL,
   'author' varchar(256) NOT NULL,
   'isbn' varchar(256) NOT NULL,
   PRIMARY KEY ('id')
) ENGINE=InnoDB AUTO_INCREMENT=1 DEFAULT CHARSET=latin1;
CREATE TABLE 'member' (
   'id' int(11) NOT NULL auto_increment,
   'first_name' varchar(256) NOT NULL,
   'last_name' varchar(256) NOT NULL,
   PRIMARY KEY ('id')
) ENGINE=InnoDB AUTO_INCREMENT=1 DEFAULT CHARSET=latin1;
CREATE TABLE 'borrowing' (
   'member_id' int(11) NOT NULL,
   'book_id' int(11) NOT NULL,
   'start_date' date NOT NULL,
   'end_date' date default NULL,
   PRIMARY KEY ('member_id','book_id'),
   KEY 'book_id' ('book_id'),
   CONSTRAINT 'borrowing_ibfk_2' FOREIGN KEY ('book_id') REFERENCES
'book' ('id'),
   CONSTRAINT `borrowing_ibfk_1` FOREIGN KEY ('member_id') REFERENCES
'member' ('id')
) ENGINE=InnoDB DEFAULT CHARSET=latin1;
```

You can create a database named library in your MySQL database and create the tables within that database using the above SQL create statements. Note that both book and member tables have a field named id as the primary key, which is of type integer. The borrowing table would have the information of the books borrowed by a member. Note that the primary key of the borrowing table is the combination of the member ID and book ID, which are foreign keys of member and book tables. The foreign key constrains on the book_id and member_id ensures data integrity. On one hand, the constraint on book_id ensures that a member would not be able to borrow a book that is not registered in the book table. On the other hand, the constraint on the member_id ensures that a person not registered in the member table cannot borrow a book.

You can use MySQL manual at http://dev.mysql.com/doc/refman /5.0/en/index.html to learn more on MySQL and use phpMyAdmin (http://www.phpmyadmin.net/) tool to help you with database management.

The design of the `borrowing` table assumes that a member borrows a given book only once. In other words, once borrowed and returned, a member cannot borrow the same book. This again is done to keep the system simple but could be changed by changing the foreign key to include the borrowing start date. Note that this assumption was made to ensure that we keep the implementation simple so that we could focus more on the application of REST principles in the PHP sample implementation that follows.

Web Page from Data

You must be familiar with PHP and with MySQL programming. Use a tool and add a couple of books to the `book` table. You can either use a visual tool like phpMyAdmin or use the MySQL command line tool. You can use the following SQL statements to insert some test data to `book` table of the library database.

```
INSERT INTO `book`
VALUES (1,'Book1','Auth1','ISBN0001'),
       (2,'Book2','Auth2','ISBN0002');
```

Now you may be familiar with the techniques to pull data from a database and prepare an HTML page out of it. Just to recap, let's see how to display the book data with an HTML page. Note that this has nothing to do with the REST sample implementation we are going to look into, but it's just to remind you of some concepts.

```php
<?php
// Connect to database
$link = mysql_connect('localhost', 'sam', 'pass') or die('Could not
connect: ' . mysql_error());
mysql_select_db('library') or die('Could not select database');

// Prepare the query, and execute the query
$query = 'SELECT b.name, b.author, b.isbn FROM book as b';
$result = mysql_query($query) or die('Query failed: ' . mysql_
error());

// Write the table headers
echo "<table border='1'>\n";
$line = mysql_fetch_assoc($result);
if ($line == null)
    return;
echo "\t<tr>\n";
foreach ($line as $key => $col_value) {
    echo "\t\t<td>$key</td>\n";
}
echo "\t</tr>\n";
// Write the data into the table
```

```
mysql_data_seek($result, 0);
while ($line = mysql_fetch_array($result, MYSQL_ASSOC)) {
    echo "\t<tr>\n";
    foreach ($line as $key => $col_value) {
        echo "\t\t<td>$col_value</td>\n";
    }
    echo "\t</tr>\n";
}
echo "</table>\n";
// Free the results and close database connection
mysql_free_result($result);
mysql_close($link);
?>
```

This script, when accessed with a Web browser, would display a table like the following:

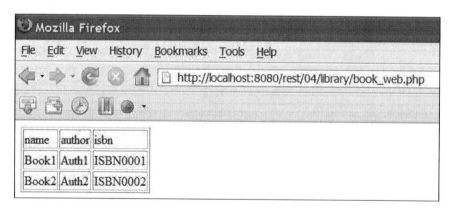

Now we are interested in implementing services rather than displaying data. However, the concepts used in this script are going to be useful while implementing services.

First we connect to the library database on the local machine with user name sam and password pass.

```
// Connect to database
$link = mysql_connect('localhost', 'sam', 'pass') or die('Could not
connect: ' . mysql_error());
mysql_select_db('library') or die('Could not select database');
```

We will use the above segment of code in our PHP service scripts to connect to the library database.

Then we prepare a query and execute that query. In this example, we select the `book name`, `author` and `ISBN` information.

```
// Prepare the query, and execute the query
$query = 'SELECT b.name, b.author, b.isbn FROM book as b';
$result = mysql_query($query) or die('Query failed: ' . mysql_error())
```

We will use similar statements to retrieve and store data to and from the library database in our service scripts.

Once the query is executed, we need to fetch data from the results structure.

```
$line = mysql_fetch_assoc($result);
```

We can use a while loop to fetch each line in the results set and deal with each result.

```
while ($line = mysql_fetch_array($result, MYSQL_ASSOC)) {
    echo "\t<tr>\n";
    foreach ($line as $key => $col_value) {
        echo "\t\t<td>$col_value</td>\n";
    }
    echo "\t</tr>\n";
}
```

We will use a similar sequence of statements to fetch data in the service scripts.

Finally, it is always a good practice to clean-up stuff after we are done with our task. So free the result set and also close the database connection.

```
// Free the results and close database connection
mysql_free_result($result);
mysql_close($link);
```

Retrieve Operation

Let's first look at how to retrieve book information from the library service. As we have already discussed, the resource URI for book is `/book`. And with GET verb, we would return all the books we have.

Here is the PHP script to retrieve the book information.

```
<?php
$link = mysql_connect('localhost', 'sam', 'pass') or die('Could not
connect: ' . mysql_error());
mysql_select_db('library') or die('Could not select database');

header("Content-Type: text/xml");

if ($_SERVER['REQUEST_METHOD'] == 'GET') {
```

```
// Handle GET request. Return the list of books.
$query = 'SELECT b.id, b.name, b.author, b.isbn FROM book as b';
$result = mysql_query($query) or die('Query failed: ' . mysql_
error());
    echo "<books>";
    while ($line = mysql_fetch_array($result, MYSQL_ASSOC)) {
        echo "<book>";
        foreach ($line as $key => $col_value) {
            echo "<$key>$col_value</$key>";
        }
        echo "</book>";
    }
    echo "</books>";

    mysql_free_result($result);
}
mysql_close($link);

?>
```

The output generated is shown in following illustration. First we connect to the database, as explained in the previous section. Then we check if the request method is HTTP GET.

```
if ($_SERVER['REQUEST_METHOD'] == 'GET')
```

If the request method is GET, we execute the select query on the book table.

```
$query = 'SELECT b.id, b.name, b.author, b.isbn FROM book as b';
$result = mysql_query($query) or die('Query failed: ' . mysql_
error());
```

For each line in the result, we create the XML output to be returned to the client from the service.

```
    echo "<books>";
    while ($line = mysql_fetch_array($result, MYSQL_ASSOC)) {
        echo "<book>";
        foreach ($line as $key => $col_value) {
            echo "<$key>$col_value</$key>";
        }
        echo "</book>";
    }
    echo "</books>";
```

This script, when accessed with a Web browser, or a client that uses GET method, will return an XML document that will look like the following:

```
<books>
    <book>
        <id>1</id>
        <name>Book1</name>
        <author>Auth1</author>
        <isbn>ISBN0001</isbn>
    </book>
    <book>
        <id>2</id>
        <name>Book2</name>
        <author>Auth2</author>
        <isbn>ISBN0002</isbn>
    </book>
</books>
```

Next, we need to implement the retrieve operation for a given book. As per the URI pattern design, the request URI would contain the book ID and we need to retrieve the data for the book with given ID. An example request URL for get book data business operation would look like:

```
http://localhost/rest/04/library/book.php/2
```

When we map the URI design to the implementation, both business operations get books and get book data would have to be served with book.php script. So we will add some logic to the script shown earlier to get book data for a given book.

Note that we are not using a query parameters to pass the ID of the book to the PHP script in this case. Rather, we are using the URI itself with a path separator character /. Passing parameters using ? followed by a query string is the functional programming style. It is similar to the concept of calling a function with a set of parameters. When designing resource-oriented services, it is better to focus on REST principles, where it is discouraged to use query parameters to get a job done. While using query parameters, we could lose track of resources and gradually the resource-oriented system could degenerate to a functional system.

First, we need to look into path elements to see if we have a book ID in the request path. This can be done by looking into the path information and splitting it with the / character.

```
// Check for the path elements
$path = $_SERVER['PATH_INFO'];
if ($path != null) {
    $path_params = spliti ("/", $path);
}
```

If the request was sent to http://localhost/rest/04/library/book.php/2, then $_SERVER['PATH_INFO'] would be /2 and we will have $path_params[0] would be equal to 2. If you are using a web server like **lighttpd**, you may run into problems with $_SERVER['PATH_INFO']. Please have a look at http://trac.lighttpd.net/trac/wiki/TutorialLighttpdAndPHP to know the details on how to deal with such problems.

Knowing this, we can prepare the query based on the fact, if we have more parameters in the path information or not, to pick the book ID from path information.

```
if ($path_params[1] != null) {
        $query = "SELECT b.id, b.name, b.author, b.isbn FROM
book as b WHERE b.id = $path_params[1]";
    } else {
        $query = "SELECT b.id, b.name, b.author, b.isbn FROM book as
b";
    }
```

We use the $path_params[1] variable directly in the SQL string in the above example. However, this would lead to security problems such as SQL injections. We should really convert the value to an integer before we start putting it into the SQL string to avoid SQL injections. You can find more information on SQL injection from http://www.php.net/security.database.sql-injection.

In this example, because we are expecting the ID to be of type integer, we could use settype() function to prevent SQL injection.

```
if ($path_params[1] != null) {
        settype($path_params[1], 'integer');
        $query = "SELECT b.id, b.name, b.author, b.isbn FROM book
as b WHERE b.id = $path_params[1]";
    }
```

Here is the full PHP script with these updates in place.

```
<?php
$link = mysql_connect('localhost', 'sam', 'pass') or die('Could not
connect: ' . mysql_error());
mysql_select_db('library') or die('Could not select database');
header("Content-Type: text/xml");
// Check for the path elements
$path = $_SERVER['PATH_INFO'];
if ($path != null) {
    $path_params = spliti ("/", $path);
}
if ($_SERVER['REQUEST_METHOD'] == 'GET') {
    if ($path_params[1] != null) {
```

```
        settype($path_params[1], 'integer');
      $query = "SELECT b.id, b.name, b.author, b.isbn FROM book as b
WHERE b.id = $path_params[1]";
    } else {
      $query = "SELECT b.id, b.name, b.author, b.isbn FROM book as
b";
    }
    $result = mysql_query($query) or die('Query failed: ' . mysql_
error());
    echo "<books>";
    while ($line = mysql_fetch_array($result, MYSQL_ASSOC)) {
        echo "<book>";
        foreach ($line as $key => $col_value) {
            echo "<$key>$col_value</$key>";
        }
        echo "</book>";
    }
    echo "</books>";
    mysql_free_result($result);
}
mysql_close($link);
?>
```

Here is a sample output from this script when accessed with the Web browser using
the URL http://localhost/rest/04/library/book.php/2.

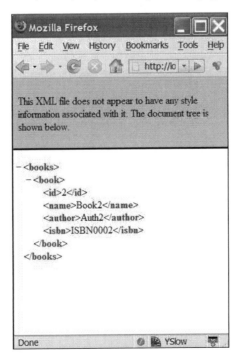

Create Operation

Again we will take the book resource to explain the implementation of `create` operation with HTTP POST verb. The URI mapping for the `get books` and `create books` is the same. Hence, we will have to use the same PHP script for implementing the `create` operation. The `retrieve` operation only needs us to specify a parameter, a `book ID`, to get a particular book, but to create a book we have to provide the data for the book as well. Hence note that the HTTP verb used is POST. So we need to check if we have received a POST request to get to know if we are supposed to insert data to the database.

```
if ($_SERVER['REQUEST_METHOD'] == 'POST') {
```

Once we have verified it is as a POST request, we have to pick the POST data and build an XML document out of that data.

```
$input = file_get_contents("php://input");
$xml = simplexml_load_string($input);
```

We assume the received input data to be of the following format:

```
<books>
    <book><name>Book3</name><author>Auth3</author><isbn>ISBN0003</
isbn></book>
    <book><name>Book4</name><author>Auth4</author><isbn>ISBN0004</
isbn></book>
</books>
```

Note that, rather than looking for a single book element, we have left the user the flexibility of creating multiple books, in other words, one or more books, with a single request.

Here is the PHP code that parses this XML document and inserts the data contained in the request to the database.

```
foreach ($xml->book as $book) {
    $query = "INSERT INTO book (name, author, isbn) VALUES
('$book->name', '$book->author', '$book->isbn')";
    $result = mysql_query($query) or die('Query failed: ' . mysql_
error());
    mysql_free_result($result);
}
```

For each book in the request payload, we insert the data into the database. Also, note that we do not expect the user to send an ID for the book while creating resource instances, rather the auto increment functionality of the database would be leveraged to generate an ID.

Here is the complete script with all retrieve and create logic in place.

```php
<?php
$link = mysql_connect('localhost', 'sam', 'pass') or die('Could not
connect: ' . mysql_error());
mysql_select_db('library') or die('Could not select database');
// Check for the path elements
$path = $_SERVER['PATH_INFO'];
if ($path != null) {
    $path_params = spliti ("/", $path);
}
if ($_SERVER['REQUEST_METHOD'] == 'POST') {
    $input = file_get_contents("php://input");
    $xml = simplexml_load_string($input);
    foreach ($xml->book as $book) {
        $query = "INSERT INTO book (name, author, isbn) VALUES
('$book->name', '$book->author', '$book->isbn')";
        $result = mysql_query($query) or die('Query failed: ' . mysql_
error());
        mysql_free_result($result);
    }
} else if ($_SERVER['REQUEST_METHOD'] == 'GET') {
    if ($path_params[1] != null) {
            $query = "SELECT b.id, b.name, b.author, b.isbn FROM
book as b WHERE b.id = $path_params[1]";
    } else {
            $query = "SELECT b.id, b.name, b.author, b.isbn FROM book as
b";
    }
    $result = mysql_query($query) or die('Query failed: ' . mysql_
error());
    echo "<books>";
    while ($line = mysql_fetch_array($result, MYSQL_ASSOC)) {
        echo "<book>";
        foreach ($line as $key => $col_value) {
            echo "<$key>$col_value</$key>";
        }
        echo "</book>";
    }
    echo "</books>";
    mysql_free_result($result);
}
mysql_close($link);
?>
```

It is the service PHP script that is provided here. As this chapter is focused on resource-oriented services, providing client code would deviate our focus. We will look into client scripts in the next chapter.

Next, let's see the script that implements the business operations that are related to the member resource. Since the concepts involved with retrieve, create and get member data are similar to those of book resource, let's look at the whole script together.

```php
<?php
$link = mysql_connect('localhost', 'sam', 'pass') or die('Could not
connect: ' . mysql_error());
mysql_select_db('library') or die('Could not select database');

$root_element_name = 'members';
$wrapper_element_name = 'member';

// Check for the path elements
$path = $_SERVER['PATH_INFO'];
if ($path != null) {
    $path_params = spliti ("/", $path);
}

if ($_SERVER['REQUEST_METHOD'] == 'POST') {
    // Handle POST request. Insert the data posted to the database.
    $input = file_get_contents("php://input");
    $xml = simplexml_load_string($input);
    foreach ($xml->member as $member) {
        $query = "INSERT INTO member (first_name, last_name) VALUES
('$member->first_name', '$member->last_name')";
        $result = mysql_query($query) or die('Query failed: ' . mysql_
error());
        mysql_free_result($result);
    }
} else if ($_SERVER['REQUEST_METHOD'] == 'GET') {
    // Handle GET request. Return the member data or the list of
members.
    if ($path_params[1] != null) {
        // Look for the given member
        $query = "SELECT m.id, m.first_name, m.last_name FROM member
as m WHERE m.id = $path_params[1]";
    } else {
        $query = "SELECT m.id, m.first_name, m.last_name FROM member
as m";
    }
    $result = mysql_query($query) or die('Query failed: ' . mysql_
error());
    echo "<$root_element_name>";
```

```
    while ($line = mysql_fetch_array($result, MYSQL_ASSOC)) {
        echo "<$wrapper_element_name>";
        foreach ($line as $key => $col_value) {
            echo "<$key>$col_value</$key>";
        }
        echo "</$wrapper_element_name>";
    }
    echo "</$root_element_name>";

    mysql_free_result($result);
}
mysql_close($link);
?>
```

You should be familiar with the concepts used in this PHP script already.

- We check if the request is a POST request and create members
- Else we check if the request is a GET request
    ◦ If path information is present, we return the data for requested member
    ◦ Else we return the list of members

Handling Multiple Path Parameters

The get member borrowings business operation would have the URI pattern /member/{member_id}/books. When mapped to the implementation, this will look something similar to:

```
http://localhost/rest/04/library/member.php/1/books
```

A GET request sent to the above URL would return the list of borrowings by member with ID 1.

As we have already seen, we can use the following logic to pick the values in path information.

```
// Check for the path elements
$path = $_SERVER['PATH_INFO'];
if ($path != null) {
    $path_params = spliti ("/", $path);
}
```

If the request URL is `http://localhost/rest/04/library/member.php/1/books`
and you do a

```
print_r($path_params);
```

You will get the output:

```
Array
(
    [0] =>
    [1] => 1
    [2] => books
)
```

We can use the following piece of logic to pick the path information and prepare the
query to be executed accordingly.

```
if ($path_params[1] != null) {
    if ($path_params[2] != null) {
        if ($path_params[2] == 'books') {
            // GET books borrowed by member
            $query = "SELECT b.id, b.name, b.author, b.isbn,
br.start_date, br.end_date FROM member as m, book as b, borrowing as
br WHERE br.member_id = m.id AND br.book_id = b.id AND m.id = $path_
params[1]";
            $root_element_name = 'books';
            $wrapper_element_name = 'book';
        }
    } else {
        $query = "SELECT m.id, m.first_name, m.last_name FROM
member as m WHERE m.id = $path_params[1]";
    }
} else {
    $query = 'SELECT m.id, m.first_name, m.last_name FROM member as
m';
}
```

This will return an XML document similar to:

```
<books>
    <book>
        <id>2</id>
        <name>Book2</name>
        <author>Auth2</author>
        <isbn>ISBN0002</isbn>
        <start_date>2008-06-16</start_date>
        <end_date></end_date>
    </book>
</books>
```

If there are path parameters and if the third element is books, then we return the list of borrowed books by the member with the ID containing $path_params[1]. This requires dealing with multiple nested IF-checks. An alternative approach would be to use a regular expression check where the path information is matched on a common term that we are looking for. As an example, this could be done in the following manner.

```php
if (ereg("books", $path)) {
    // GET books borrowed by member
    $query = "SELECT b.id, b.name, b.author, b.isbn FROM
member as m, book as b, borrowing as br WHERE br.member_id = m.id AND
br.book_id = b.id AND m.id = $path_params[1]";
    $root_element_name = 'books';
    $wrapper_element_name = 'book';
}
```

Next, let's look into the borrow book business operation. The URI pattern for this operation is /member/{member_id}/books/{book_id}. When mapped to the implementation, this will look something similar to:

```
http://localhost/rest/04/library/member.php/1/books/2
```

With the above URL, if you do a

```php
print_r($path_params);
```

You will get the output:

```
Array
(
    [0] =>
    [1] => 1
    [2] => books
    [3] => 2
)
```

When a POST request comes to this endpoint, what it means is that, member with ID 1 borrows book with ID 2. Here is the PHP code for looking into the parameters and creating a new book borrowing record.

```php
if ($path_params[1] != null && $path_params[2] != null && $path_params[3] != null) {
    if ($path_params[2] == 'books') {
        // a book being borrowed by member
        $today = date("Y-m-d");
        $query = "INSERT INTO borrowing (member_id, book_id,
start_date) VALUES ($path_params[1], $path_params[3], '$today')";
```

```
        $result = mysql_query($query) or die('Query failed: ' .
mysql_error());
            mysql_free_result($result);
        }
    }
```

This code picks up the member ID and book ID from path information and creates a booking with start date set to today. Note that this would be inside the block where a POST request is processed.

The return book operation would be implemented for the same URL pattern, but with the HTTP method DELETE.

```
    if ($_SERVER['REQUEST_METHOD'] == 'DELETE') {
        // Handle POST request. Insert the data posted to the database.
        if ($path_params[1] != null && $path_params[2] != null && $path_
params[3] != null) {
            if ($path_params[2] == 'books') {
                // a book being borrowed by member
                $today = date("Y-m-d");
                echo $today;
                $query = "Update borrowing as br SET end_date = '$today'
where br.member_id = $path_params[1] and br.book_id = $path_
params[3]";
                echo $query;
                $result = mysql_query($query) or die('Query failed: ' .
mysql_error());
                mysql_free_result($result);
            }
        }
    }
```

This code picks up the member ID and book ID from path information and updates the booking with end date set to today.

Here is the complete source code for member.php script, where all of following business operations are included:

- List members
- Create member(s)
- Get member data
- List borrowings
- Borrow book
- Return book

```php
<?php
function init_database() {
    $link = mysql_connect('localhost', 'sam', 'pass') or die('Could
not connect: ' . mysql_error());
    mysql_select_db('library') or die('Could not select database');
    return $link;
}


function handle_borrow_book($member_id, $book_id) {
    $today = date("Y-m-d");
    $query = "INSERT INTO borrowing (member_id, book_id, start_date)
VALUES ($member_id, $book_id, '$today')";
    $result = mysql_query($query) or die('Query failed: ' . mysql_
error());
    mysql_free_result($result);
}


function add_member() {
    $input = file_get_contents("php://input");
    $xml = simplexml_load_string($input);
    foreach ($xml->member as $member) {
        $query = "INSERT INTO member (first_name, last_name) VALUES
('$member->first_name', '$member->last_name')";
        $result = mysql_query($query) or die('Query failed: ' . mysql_
error());
        mysql_free_result($result);
    }
}


function print_result($query, $root_element_name, $wrapper_element_
name) {
    $result = mysql_query($query) or die('Query failed: ' . mysql_
error());
    echo "<$root_element_name>";
    while ($line = mysql_fetch_array($result, MYSQL_ASSOC)) {
        echo "<$wrapper_element_name>";
        foreach ($line as $key => $col_value) {
            echo "<$key>$col_value</$key>";
        }
        echo "</$wrapper_element_name>";
    }
    echo "</$root_element_name>";
    mysql_free_result($result);
}

function get_books_borrowed($member_id) {
```

```
    $query = "SELECT b.id, b.name, b.author, b.isbn, br.start_date,
br.end_date FROM member as m, book as b, borrowing as br WHERE
br.member_id = m.id AND br.book_id = b.id AND m.id = $member_id AND
br.end_date is NULL";
    $root_element_name = 'books';
    $wrapper_element_name = 'book';
    print_result($query, $root_element_name, $wrapper_element_name);
}


function get_member($member_id) {
    $query = "SELECT m.id, m.first_name, m.last_name FROM member as m
WHERE m.id = $member_id";
    $root_element_name = 'members';
    $wrapper_element_name = 'member';
    print_result($query, $root_element_name, $wrapper_element_name);
}


function get_members() {
    $query = "SELECT m.id, m.first_name, m.last_name FROM member as
m";
    $root_element_name = 'members';
    $wrapper_element_name = 'member';
    print_result($query, $root_element_name, $wrapper_element_name);
}


function handle_return_book($member_id, $book_id) {
    $today = date("Y-m-d");
    $query = "Update borrowing as br SET end_date = '$today' where
br.member_id = $member_id and br.book_id = $book_id";
    $result = mysql_query($query) or die('Query failed: ' . mysql_
error());
    mysql_free_result($result);
}


$database = init_database();


// Set the content type to text/xml
header("Content-Type: text/xml");


// Check for the path elements
$path = $_SERVER[PATH_INFO];
if ($path != null) {
    $path_params = spliti("/", $path);
}

if ($_SERVER['REQUEST_METHOD'] == 'POST') {
```

```php
        // Handle POST request. Insert the data posted to the database.
    if ($path_params[1] != null && $path_params[2] != null && $path_
params[3] != null) {
        if ($path_params[2] == 'books') {
            // a book being borrowed by member
            handle_borrow_book($path_params[1], $path_params[3]);
        }
    } else {
        add_member();
    }
} else
    if ($_SERVER['REQUEST_METHOD'] == 'GET') {
        // Handle GET request. Return the list of members.
        if ($path_params[1] != null) {
            if ($path_params[2] != null) {
                if ($path_params[2] == 'books') {
                    // GET books borrowed by member
                    get_books_borrowed($path_params[1]);
                }
            } else {
                // GET member details for given ID
                get_member($path_params[1]);
            }
        } else {
            // GET all members
            get_members();
        }
    } else
        if ($_SERVER['REQUEST_METHOD'] == 'DELETE') {
            // Handle DELETE request. Handle the book return
operation.
            if ($path_params[1] != null && $path_params[2] != null &&
$path_params[3] != null) {
                if ($path_params[2] == 'books') {
                    // a book being returned by member
                    handle_return_book($path_params[1], $path_
params[3]);
                }
            }
        }
mysql_close($database);
?>
```

Summary

This chapter covered the steps that you would have to follow in designing and implementing a resource-oriented service, in detail. Identifying resources and business operations for a given problem statement, designing the URI patterns, selecting the correct HTTP verbs, mapping URI and HTTP verbs to business operations were covered using the library example. Implementing the services and business operations using PHP was explained in detail, step by step.

In the next chapter, we will cover how to implement resource-oriented clients using PHP for the library example introduced in this chapter.

5
Resource-Oriented Clients

Resource-Oriented clients are client programs that consume services designed in accordance with the REST architectural principles. As explained in Chapter 1, the key REST principles include:

- The concept of resource (for example, a document is a resource)
- Every resource given a unique ID (for example, document URL)
- Resources can be related (for example, One document linking to another)
- Use of standard (HTTP, HTML, XML)
- Resources can have multiple forms (for example, status of a document, updated, validated, deleted)
- Communicate in a stateless fashion using HTTP (for example, subsequent requests not related to each other)

In the previous chapter, we studied in detail, and from ground-up, how to design and implement services to comply with REST architectural principles. In this chapter, we will study how we can implement clients to consume those services. We will use the same real-world example that we used in the last chapter, the simplified library system, to learn from scratch how to design clients with REST principles in mind.

Designing Clients

In the last chapter, while designing the library service, the ultimate outcome was the mapping of business operations to URIs and HTTP verbs. The client design is governed by this mapping.

Prior to service design, the problem statement was analysed. For consuming the service and invoking the business operations of the service using clients, there needs to be some understanding of how the service intends to solve the problem. In other words, the service, by design, has already solved the problem. However, the semantics of the solution provided by the service needs to be understood by the developers implementing the clients. The semantics of the service is usually documented in terms of business operations and the relationships between those operations. And sometimes, the semantics are obvious. As an example, in the library system, a member returning a book must have already borrowed that book. The `borrow book` operation precedes the `return book` operation. Client design must take these semantics into account.

Resource Design

Following is the URI and HTTP verb mapping for business operations of the library system that we came up with in the last chapter.

URI	HTTP Method	Collection	Operation	Business Operation
/book	GET	books	retrieve	Get books
/book	POST	books	create	Add book(s)
/book/{book_id}	GET	books	retrieve	Get book data
/member	GET	members	retrieve	Get members
/member	POST	members	create	Add member(s)
/member/{member_id}	GET	members	retrieve	Get member data
/member/{member_id}/books	GET	members	retrieve	Get member borrowings
/member/{member_id}/ books/{book_id}	POST	members	create	Borrow book
/member/{member_id}/ books/{book_id}	DELETE	members	delete	Return book

When it comes to client design, the resource design is given, and is an input to the client design. The resource design was covered in the last chapter where we designed the service design. When it comes to implementing clients, we have to adhere to the design given to us by the service designer. In this example, we designed the API given in the above table, so we are already familiar with the API. Sometimes, you may have to use an API designed by someone else, hence you would have to ensure that you have access to information such as:

- Resource URI formats
- HTTP methods involved with each resource URI
- The resource collection that is associated with the URI
- The nature of the operation to be executed combining the URI and the HTTP verb
- The business operation that maps the resource operation to the real world context

Looking into the above resource design table, we can identify two resources, book and member. And we could understand some of the semantics associated with the business operations of the resources.

- Create, retrieve books
- Create, retrieve members
- Borrow book, list borrowed books and return book
- Book ID and member ID could be used to invoke operations specific to a particular book or member instance

System Implementation

In this section, we will use the techniques that we discussed in the previous chapters on client programming to consume the library service we implemented in the last chapter. These techniques include:

- Building requests using XML
- Sending requests with correct HTTP verbs using an HTTP client library like CURL
- Receiving XML responses and processing the received responses to extract information that we require from the response

Retrieving Resource Information

Here is the PHP source code to retrieve book information.

```php
<?php
$url = 'http://localhost/rest/04/library/book.php';

$client = curl_init($url);
curl_setopt($client, CURLOPT_RETURNTRANSFER, 1);
$response = curl_exec($client);
curl_close($client);
```

```php
$xml = simplexml_load_string($response);

foreach ($xml->book as $book) {
    echo "$book->id, $book->name, $book->author, $book->isbn <br/>\n";
}
?>
```

The output generated is shown below.

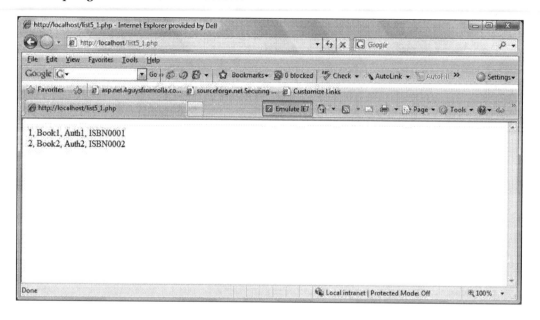

As per the service design, all that is required is to send a GET request to the URL of the book resource. And as per the service semantics, we are expecting the response to be something similar to:

```xml
<books>
    <book>
        <id>1</id>
        <name>Book1</name>
        <author>Auth1</author>
        <isbn>ISBN0001</isbn>
    </book>
    <book>
        <id>2</id>
        <name>Book2</name>
        <author>Auth2</author>
        <isbn>ISBN0002</isbn>
    </book>
</books>
```

So in the client, we convert the response to an XML tree.

```
$xml = simplexml_load_string($response);
```

And generate the output that we desire from the client. In this case we print all the books.

```
foreach ($xml->book as $book) {
    echo "$book->id, $book->name, $book->author, $book->isbn <br/>\n";
}
```

The output is:

```
1, Book1, Auth1, ISBN0001
2, Book2, Auth2, ISBN0002
```

Similarly, we could retrieve all the members with the following PHP script.

```
<?php
$url = 'http://localhost/rest/04/library/member.php';
$client = curl_init($url);
curl_setopt($client, CURLOPT_RETURNTRANSFER, 1);
$response = curl_exec($client);
curl_close($client);
$xml = simplexml_load_string($response);
foreach ($xml->member as $member) {
    echo "$member->id, $member->first_name, $member->last_name <br/>\
n";
}
?>
```

Next, retrieving books borrowed by a member.

```
<?php
$url = 'http://localhost/rest/04/library/member.php/1/books';
$client = curl_init($url);
curl_setopt($client, CURLOPT_RETURNTRANSFER, 1);
$response = curl_exec($client);
curl_close($client);
$xml = simplexml_load_string($response);
foreach ($xml->book as $book) {
    echo "$book->id, $book->name, $book->author, $book->isbn <br/>\n";
}
?>
```

Here we are retrieving the books borrowed by member with ID 1. Only the URL differs, the rest of the logic is the same.

Creating Resources

Books, members, and borrowings could be created using POST operations, as per the service design. The following PHP script creates a new book.

```php
<?php

$url = 'http://localhost/rest/04/library/book.php';

$data = <<<XML
<books>
    <book><name>Book3</name><author>Auth3</author><isbn>ISBN0003</isbn></book>
    <book><name>Book4</name><author>Auth4</author><isbn>ISBN0004</isbn></book>
</books>
XML;

$ch = curl_init();

curl_setopt($ch, CURLOPT_URL, $url);
curl_setopt($ch, CURLOPT_RETURNTRANSFER, true);
curl_setopt($ch, CURLOPT_POST, true);
curl_setopt($ch, CURLOPT_POSTFIELDS, $data);

$response = curl_exec($ch);

curl_close($ch);

echo $response;
?>
```

When data is sent with POST verb to the URI of the book resource, the posted data would be used to create resource instances. Note that, in order to figure out the format of the XML message to be used, you have to look into the service operation documentation. This is where the knowledge on service semantics comes into play.

Next is the PHP script to create members.

```php
<?php

$url = 'http://localhost/rest/04/library/member.php';

$data = <<<XML
<members><member><first_name>Sam</first_name><last_name>Noel</last_name></member></members>
XML;

$ch = curl_init();

curl_setopt($ch, CURLOPT_URL, $url);
curl_setopt($ch, CURLOPT_RETURNTRANSFER, true);
curl_setopt($ch, CURLOPT_POST, true);
```

```
curl_setopt($ch, CURLOPT_POSTFIELDS, $data);

$response = curl_exec($ch);

curl_close($ch);

echo $response;
?>
```

This script is very similar to the script that creates books. Only differences are the endpoint address and the XML payload used. The endpoint address refers to the location where the service is located. In the above script the endpoint address of the service is:

```
$url = 'http://localhost/rest/04/library/member.php';
```

Next, borrowing a book can be done by posting to the member URI with the ID of the member borrowing the book, and the ID of the book being borrowed.

```
<?php
$url = 'http://localhost/rest/04/library/member.php/1/books/2';

$data = <<<XML
XML;

$ch = curl_init();
curl_setopt($ch, CURLOPT_URL, $url);
curl_setopt($ch, CURLOPT_RETURNTRANSFER, true);
curl_setopt($ch, CURLOPT_POST, true);
curl_setopt($ch, CURLOPT_POSTFIELDS, $data);

$response = curl_exec($ch);

curl_close($ch);

echo $response;
?>
```

Note that, in the above sample, we are not posting any data to the URI. Hence the XML payload is empty:

```
$data = <<<XML
XML;
```

As per the REST architectural principles, we just send a POST request with all resource information on the URI itself. In this example, the member with ID 1 is borrowing the book with ID 2.

```
$url = 'http://localhost/rest/04/library/member.php/1/books/2';
```

One of the things to be noted in the client scripts is that we have used hard coded URLs and parameter values. When you are using these scripts with an application that uses a Web-based user interface, those hard coded values need to be parameterized.

And we send a POST request to this URL:

```
curl_setopt($ch, CURLOPT_URL, $url);
curl_setopt($ch, CURLOPT_RETURNTRANSFER, true);
curl_setopt($ch, CURLOPT_POST, true);
curl_setopt($ch, CURLOPT_POSTFIELDS, $data);
```

Note that, even though the XML payload that we are sending to the service is empty, we still have to set the CURLOPT_POSTFIELDS option for CURL. This is because we have set CURLOPT_POST to true and the CRUL library mandates setting POST field option even when it is empty.

This script would cause a book borrowing to be created on the server side. As we saw in the last chapter, when the member.php script receives a request with the from /{member_id}/books/{book_id} with HTTP verb POST, it maps the request to borrow book business operation. So, the URL

```
$url = 'http://localhost/rest/04/library/member.php/1/books/2';
```

means that member with ID 1 is borrowing the book with ID 2.

Deleting Resources

We can use the HTTP DELETE operation to return the book.

```
<?php
$url = 'http://localhost/rest/04/library/member.php/1/books/2';
$ch = curl_init();
curl_setopt($ch, CURLOPT_URL, $url);
curl_setopt($ch, CURLOPT_CUSTOMREQUEST, "DELETE");
curl_exec($ch);
curl_close($ch);
?>
```

In this case, we are sending a DELETE request with member ID and book ID in place. The above script indicates that member with ID 1 is returning the book with ID 2.

Putting it All Together

Writing the client scripts is trivial, all you have to do is:

- Identify the endpoint URI
- Find out the XML message format to be sent to service, if any
- Identify the expected HTTP verb to be used
- Send request
- Process response

Steps 1 to 3 would be found in service API documentation. In our example library system, we used a table to document our service API:

URI	HTTP Method	Collection	Operation	Business Operation
/book	GET	books	retrieve	Get books
/book	POST	books	create	Add book(s)

As we have seen in the previous chapters, all popular publicly available Web services have documentation available and those documents contain all these information.

Steps 4 and 5 consist of the use of HTTP client libraries and XML processing that we discussed in Chapter 2.

Implementing a Form-based Application

So far, we looked into the elements of PHP source code that would let us access the various operations of the library system. Now, let's see how we could put them all together.

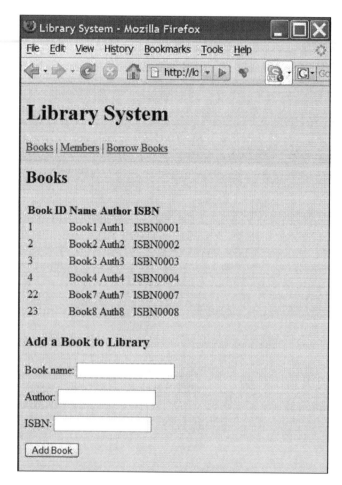

The above picture shows an application built on top of the service interface provided by the library system. The main menu of this application is right below the main page title. You can view and add books, view and add members as well as borrow books and list the books borrowed by members. This application consists of one HTML file and three PHP scripts. The HTML file forms the main layout of the application.

Here is the index HTML file.

```
<!DOCTYPE HTML PUBLIC "-//W3C//DTD HTML 4.01 Transitional//EN"
"http://www.w3.org/TR/html4/loose.dtd">
<html>
<head>
    <meta http-equiv="content-type" content="text/html; charset=UTF-8">
    <title>Library System</title>

    <script language="javascript">
    <!--
    function fillContent(resource)
    {
        xmlhttp = new XMLHttpRequest();
        xmlhttp.open("GET", resource, true);
        xmlhttp.onreadystatechange=function() {
            if (xmlhttp.readyState==4) {
                document.getElementById('content').innerHTML = xmlhttp.
responseText;
            }
        }
        xmlhttp.send(null);
    }
    -->
    </script>
</head>
<body onload="fillContent('books.php')">
    <h1>Library System</h1>
    <div id="menu" align="left"><a href="#" onclick="javascript:
fillContent('books.php')">Books</a>
    | <a href="#" onclick="javascript:fillContent('members.
php')">Members</a>
    | <a href="#" onclick="javascript:fillContent('borrowings.
php')">Borrow Books</a>
    </div>

    <div id="content" align="left">
    </div>
</body>
</html>
```

This HTML code divides the browser window into two `div` areas, with the Ids `menu` and `content`.

The `div` section with the ID `menu`, displays the menu.

```
    <div id="menu" align="left"><a href="#" onclick="javascript:
fillContent('books.php')">Books</a>
    | <a href="#" onclick="javascript:fillContent('members.
php')">Members</a>
    | <a href="#" onclick="javascript:fillContent('borrowings.
php')">Borrow Books</a>
    </div>
```

Note that each menu item is linked to a JavaScript `onclick` action. The JavaScript action calls the JavaScript function `fillContent()` with the name of the PHP script to be loaded to the content `div`.

The `fillContent()` JavaScript function creates an `XMLHttpRequest` object instance and send a GET request to the PHP resource to load HTML content to the content `div`.

```
    xmlhttp = new XMLHttpRequest();
    xmlhttp.open("GET", resource, true);
```

Then once the content is received, when the `XMLHttpRequest` object's state changes to ready, the response text received is set as the inner HTML of the content div.

```
    xmlhttp.onreadystatechange=function() {
        if (xmlhttp.readyState==4) {
            document.getElementById('content').innerHTML = xmlhttp.
responseText;
        }
    }
```

Let us look at the PHP script that handles books.

We need to list the books and display them in a table. The following code does that.

```
    <table>
    <tr>
      <th> Book ID </th>
      <th> Name </th>
      <th> Author </th>
      <th> ISBN </th>
    </tr>
<!-- List Books -->
<?php

$url = 'http://localhost/rest/04/library/book.php';

$client = curl_init($url);
curl_setopt($client, CURLOPT_RETURNTRANSFER, 1);
$response = curl_exec($client);
```

```php
curl_close($client);

$xml = simplexml_load_string($response);

foreach ($xml->book as $book) {
    echo "<tr> <td> $book->id </td> <td> $book->name </td> <td> $book->author </td> <td>$book->isbn </td></tr>";
}
?>
    </table>
```

We also need to have a form to facilitate the addition of a new book. Here is the source code for the form.

```html
<h2> Add a Book to Library </h2>

<form>
    <form action="books.php" method="POST">
        <p>Book name: <input type="text" name="name" /></p>
        <p>Author: <input type="text" name="author" /></p>
        <p>ISBN: <input type="text" name="isbn" /></p>
        <p><input type="submit" name="submit" value="Add Book" /></p>
    </form>
```

Now once the **Submit** button is clicked by the user, we post that data to the same PHP script, so the `create book` operation needs to be handled by the same PHP script. Now that needs to be done before we list the books, as we would like the new book too to appear in the list of books. Following is the PHP source code to do this.

```php
<?php
if (isset ($_GET['name'])) {

    $url = 'http://localhost/rest/04/library/book.php';

    $data = "<books><book><name>" . $_GET['name'] . "</name><author>" . $_GET['author'] .
    "</author><isbn>" . $_GET['isbn'] . "</isbn></book></books>";

    $ch = curl_init();

    curl_setopt($ch, CURLOPT_URL, $url);
    curl_setopt($ch, CURLOPT_RETURNTRANSFER, true);
    curl_setopt($ch, CURLOPT_POST, true);
    curl_setopt($ch, CURLOPT_POSTFIELDS, $data);

    $response = curl_exec($ch);

    curl_close($ch);
}
?>
```

This code looks if the `name` parameter is set,

```
if (isset ($_GET['name'])) {
```

And if it is set, we know that the user submits a request for a new book creation. So we pick the name, author, and ISBN from the parameters and from the data string to be posted for the `create book` operation.

```
$data = "<books><book><name>" . $_GET['name'] . "</name><author>"
. $_GET['author'] .
    "</author><isbn>" . $_GET['isbn'] . "</isbn></book></books>";
```

Following is the full source code for this `books.php` script.

```
<!DOCTYPE HTML PUBLIC "-//W3C//DTD HTML 4.01 Transitional//EN"
"http://www.w3.org/TR/html4/loose.dtd">
<html>
<head>
  <meta http-equiv="content-type" content="text/html; charset=UTF-8">
</head>
<body>

<!-- Create book -->
<?php
if (isset ($_GET['name'])) {

    $url = 'http://localhost/rest/04/library/book.php';

    $data = "<books><book><name>" . $_GET['name'] . "</name><author>"
. $_GET['author'] .
    "</author><isbn>" . $_GET['isbn'] . "</isbn></book></books>";

    $ch = curl_init();

    curl_setopt($ch, CURLOPT_URL, $url);
    curl_setopt($ch, CURLOPT_RETURNTRANSFER, true);
    curl_setopt($ch, CURLOPT_POST, true);
    curl_setopt($ch, CURLOPT_POSTFIELDS, $data);

    $response = curl_exec($ch);

    curl_close($ch);
}
?>

    <h2>Books</h2>
    <table>
    <tr>
      <th> Book ID </th>
      <th> Name </th>
      <th> Author </th>
```

```
            <th> ISBN </th>
        </tr>
<!-- List Books -->
<?php

$url = 'http://localhost/rest/04/library/book.php';

$client = curl_init($url);
curl_setopt($client, CURLOPT_RETURNTRANSFER, 1);
$response = curl_exec($client);
curl_close($client);

$xml = simplexml_load_string($response);

foreach ($xml->book as $book) {
    echo "<tr> <td> " . htmlspecialchars($book->id) . "</td> ".
        " <td> " . htmlspecialchars($book->name) . "</td> " .
        " <td> " . htmlspecialchars($book->author) . " </td> ".
        " <td> " . htmlspecialchars($book->isbn) . " </td></tr>";
}
?>

    </table>

    <h3> Add a Book to Library </h3>

    <form>
        <form action="books.php" method="POST">
            <p>Book name: <input type="text" name="name" /></p>
            <p>Author: <input type="text" name="author" /></p>
            <p>ISBN: <input type="text" name="isbn" /></p>
            <p><input type="submit" name="submit" value="Add Book"
/></p>
    </form>
</body>
</html>
```

The members.php script does more or less the same job. It lists members and lets you add a new member.

Here is the full source code:

```
<!DOCTYPE HTML PUBLIC "-//W3C//DTD HTML 4.01 Transitional//EN"
"http://www.w3.org/TR/html4/loose.dtd">
<html>
<head>
    <meta http-equiv="content-type" content="text/html; charset=UTF-8">
</head>
<body>
```

```php
<!-- Add member -->
<?php
if (isset ($_GET['fname'])) {

    $url = 'http://localhost/rest/04/library/member.php';

    $data = "<members><member><first_name>" . $_GET['fname'] . "</
first_name><last_name>" .
            $_GET['lname'] . "</last_name></member></members>";

    $ch = curl_init();

    curl_setopt($ch, CURLOPT_URL, $url);
    curl_setopt($ch, CURLOPT_RETURNTRANSFER, true);
    curl_setopt($ch, CURLOPT_POST, true);
    curl_setopt($ch, CURLOPT_POSTFIELDS, $data);

    $response = curl_exec($ch);

    curl_close($ch);
}
?>

<!-- List members -->
   <h2>Members</h2>
   <table>
   <tr>
     <th> Member ID </th>
     <th> First Name </th>
     <th> Last Name </th>
   </tr>
<?php

$url = 'http://localhost/rest/04/library/member.php';

$client = curl_init($url);
curl_setopt($client, CURLOPT_RETURNTRANSFER, 1);
$response = curl_exec($client);
curl_close($client);

$xml = simplexml_load_string($response);

foreach ($xml->member as $member) {
    echo "<tr> <td> ". htmlspecialchars($member->id) . " </td> " .
        " <td> " . htmlspecialchars($member->first_name) . " </td> "
.
        " <td> " . htmlspecialchars($member->last_name) . " </td> </
tr>";
}
?>
   </table>

   <!-- Display the form -->
```

```
<h3> Add a Member </h3>
<form>
    <form action="members.php" method="POST">
        <p>First name: <input type="text" name="fname" /></p>
        <p>Last name: <input type="text" name="lname" /></p>
        <p><input type="submit" name="submit" value="Add Member"
/></p>
    </form>
</body>
</html>
```

The three main sections of this code are clearly marked with comments and are identical to those that we saw in the `books.php` script.

- Add member
- List members
- Display add member form

Here is what we would see on the display.

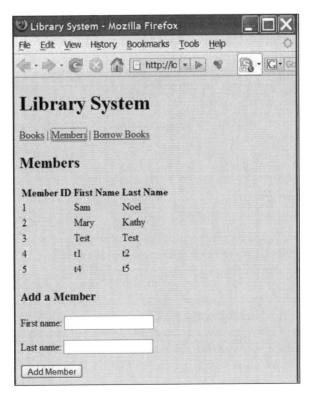

Finally, we have the `borrowings.php script`. This script displays the borrowings done by a member and also has a form that lets us borrow or return a book, providing the book ID and the member ID.

This script is slightly different from the books and members script of this client application. Listing the borrowings needs two resources to be accessed.

```php
<?php
$url = 'http://localhost/rest/04/library/member.php';
$client = curl_init($url);
curl_setopt($client, CURLOPT_RETURNTRANSFER, 1);
$response = curl_exec($client);
curl_close($client);
$xml = simplexml_load_string($response);
foreach ($xml->member as $member) {
    echo "<tr> <td> $member->id </td> <td> $member->first_name </td>
<td> $member->last_name </td>";

    $url = "http://localhost/rest/04/library/member.php/$member->id/
books";

    $client = curl_init($url);
    curl_setopt($client, CURLOPT_RETURNTRANSFER, 1);
    $response = curl_exec($client);
    curl_close($client);

    $xml = simplexml_load_string($response);

    foreach ($xml->book as $book) {
        echo "<td> $book->id , $book->name</td>";
    }
    echo "</tr>";
}
?>
```

There are two `foreach` loops in this section of code. The outer loop accesses the list of members and lists them, while the inner loop access the borrowed books for that member and lists them.

In a functional design approach, access of the members and the books borrowed by a given member would have been broken into two separate functions. However, while designing a service API the information contained in a response resulting from an operation invocation would contain all applicable information which is related to that operation. This will make sure that the number of requests from client to the service would be minimized to get a business operation completed. This is considered good practice because less requests from client to service means less use of the network and that makes the application become faster.

The form in this script also is different. It has two **Submit** buttons, one for book borrowing and the other for returning.

```
<form>
    <form action="members.php" method="POST">
      <p>Member ID: <input type="text" name="m_id" /></p>
      <p>Book ID: <input type="text" name="b_id" /></p>
      <p><input type="submit" name="borrow" value="Borrow Book" />
      <input type="submit" name="return" value="Return Book" /></p>
</form>
```

Since the form can be submitted using either button, we have to take that into account while processing the submitted data.

We have to first check if it is the **borrow** button or the **return** button that was clicked.

```
if (isset ($_GET['borrow']) || isset ($_GET['return'])) {
```

And based on that, we have to either perform a POST operation for borrowing or a DELETE operation for returning the resource. The resource URL should contain the book ID and the member ID.

```
$url = "http://localhost/rest/04/library/member.php/" . $_GET['m_id']
        "/books/" . $_GET['b_id'];
```

And we pick the correct HTTP verb to be used.

```
    if (isset ($_GET['borrow'])) {
        curl_setopt($ch, CURLOPT_RETURNTRANSFER, true);
        curl_setopt($ch, CURLOPT_POST, true);
        $data = "";
        curl_setopt($ch, CURLOPT_POSTFIELDS, $data);
    } else if (isset ($_GET['return'])) {
        curl_setopt($ch, CURLOPT_CUSTOMREQUEST, "DELETE");
    }
```

Here is the output.

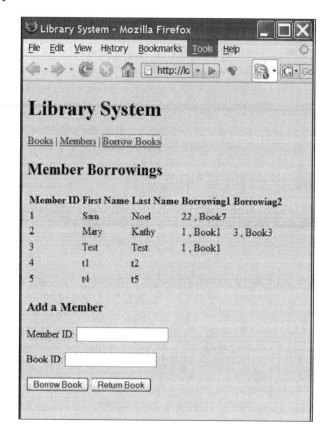

And the complete source code for the borrowings PHP script is given below.

```
<!DOCTYPE HTML PUBLIC "-//W3C//DTD HTML 4.01 Transitional//EN"
"http://www.w3.org/TR/html4/loose.dtd">
<html>
<head>
  <meta http-equiv="content-type" content="text/html; charset=UTF-8">
</head>
<body>

<!-- Handle borrow or return book operations -->
<?php
if (isset ($_GET['borrow']) || isset ($_GET['return'])) {
    $url = "http://localhost/rest/04/library/member.php/" . $_GET['m_
id'] .
        "/books/" . $_GET['b_id'];
```

```php
    $ch = curl_init();
    curl_setopt($ch, CURLOPT_URL, $url);
    if (isset($_GET['borrow'])) {
        curl_setopt($ch, CURLOPT_RETURNTRANSFER, true);
        curl_setopt($ch, CURLOPT_POST, true);
        $data = "";
        curl_setopt($ch, CURLOPT_POSTFIELDS, $data);
    } else if (isset($_GET['return'])) {
        curl_setopt($ch, CURLOPT_CUSTOMREQUEST, "DELETE");
    }
    curl_exec($ch);
    curl_close($ch);
}
?>
<!-- List book borrowings by members -->
    <h2>Member Borrowings</h2>
    <table>
    <tr>
      <th> Member ID </th>
      <th> First Name </th>
      <th> Last Name </th>
      <th> Borrowing1 </th>
      <th> Borrowing2 </th>
    </tr>
<?php
$url = 'http://localhost/rest/04/library/member.php';

$client = curl_init($url);
curl_setopt($client, CURLOPT_RETURNTRANSFER, 1);
$response = curl_exec($client);
curl_close($client);

$xml = simplexml_load_string($response);

foreach ($xml->member as $member) {
    echo "<tr> <td> " . htmlspecialchars($member->id) . " </td> ".
        "<td> " . htmlspecialchars($member->first_name) . " </td> " .
        "<td> " . htmlspecialchars($member->last_name) . " </td>";

    $url = "http://localhost/rest/04/library/member.php/$member->id/books";

    $client = curl_init($url);
    curl_setopt($client, CURLOPT_RETURNTRANSFER, 1);
    $response = curl_exec($client);
    curl_close($client);
```

```php
    $xml = simplexml_load_string($response);
    foreach ($xml->book as $book) {
        echo "<td> $book->id , $book->name</td>";
    }
    echo "</tr>";
}
?>
```

```html
    </table>

    <!-- Display the form to borrow or return books -->
    <h3> Add a Member </h3>

    <form>
        <form action="members.php" method="POST">
            <p>Member ID: <input type="text" name="m_id" /></p>
            <p>Book ID: <input type="text" name="b_id" /></p>
            <p><input type="submit" name="borrow" value="Borrow Book"
/>
            <input type="submit" name="return" value="Return Book"
/></p>
        </form>
</body>
</html>
```

Summary

This chapter covered the steps that you would have to follow in designing and implementing resource-oriented clients in detail. The design of the clients is governed by the design of the service. And the client programmer needs to understand the semantics of the service, which is usually communicated through service API documentation. In the examples of this chapter, we used the library service API that we designed in the last chapter to explain how we could use an existing API while designing PHP applications.

In the next chapter, we will look into Zend framework's REST API.

6
Resource-Oriented Clients and Services with Zend Framework

Zend framework is a PHP component library, which simplifies the building of PHP applications. It is a collection of PHP files and not a PHP extension implemented in C like **libcurl**. Zend is a company that provides commercial support for PHP, and because this framework comes from that company, it has a serious standing in the industry. The framework is available for download for free.

You can find more information on Zend Framework from http://framework.zend.com/. Zend Framework comes with PHP classes that provide APIs that are easy to use when it comes to writing REST services and clients. In this chapter, we will see how we can use the Zend framework to implement REST services and clients and will also see how we can implement the library system that was introduced the in last two chapters using the Zend Framework.

Zend Framework has been designed with simplicity in mind. It provides a lightweight, loosely-coupled component library. It can also be customized to meet specific business needs. There are no configuration files and so it is easier to get started. It is a high-quality, object-oriented PHP 5 class library that is well tested and ready to use.

Installing Zend Framework

You can download the Zend Framework from http://framework.zend.com/download. Then you can extract the contents of the library folder to the directory wherever you want to place the PHP libraries. Inside the library folder of the Zend framework extract there is a top-level Zend directory which contains all Zend Framework components.

Once you copy the library folder of Zend Framework, it is installed and ready to use.

Services with Zend_Rest_Server

The `Zend_Rest_Server` class in Zend Framework can be used to implement REST style services. You can find the PHP class API at `http://framework.zend.com/apidoc/core/Zend_Rest/Server/Zend_Rest_Server.html`.

Let's first see a simple example (`hello.php`) on how to use the `Zend_Rest_Server` class. This script acts as a service and sends a "`Hello World`" greeting in the XML payload when accessed.

```php
<?php
require_once 'Zend/Rest/Server.php';
/**
 * Say Hello
 */
function sayHello()
{
    return 'Hello World';
}
$server = new Zend_Rest_Server();
$server->addFunction('sayHello');
$server->handle();
?>
```

Run the PHP with URL `http://localhost/hello.php?method=sayHello`

The output from `hello.php` is shown below.

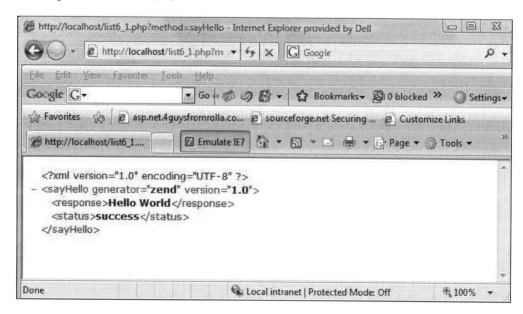

This PHP script implements a simple hello world REST style service using the `Zend_Rest_Server` class.

We would obviously require the server class.

```
require_once 'Zend/Rest/Server.php';
```

Then we define the service function. In this way we have a single function named sayHello.

```
/**
 * Say Hello
 */
function sayHello()
{
    return 'Hello World';
}
```

Next, we need to create the server class instance and add the service function.

```
$server = new Zend_Rest_Server();
$server->addFunction('sayHello');
```

Finally, we call the handle member method of the server class. Call to this function indicates that we should handle the incoming request with the function added to the service.

```
$server->handle();
```

We can send a HTTP GET request to the service using the URL `http://localhost/hello.php?method=sayHello`. Once a request is received by this service, it will call the sayHello function and get the return value of that function to form the response and send to the client. The response would be in XML format as shown below.

```
<?xml version="1.0" encoding="UTF-8"?>
<sayHello generator="zend" version="1.0">
    <response>Hello World</response>
    <status>success</status>
</sayHello>
```

Clients with Zend_Rest_Client

The `Zend_Rest_Client` class in Zend Framework can be used to implement REST style clients. You can find the PHP class API at `http://framework.zend.com/apidoc/core/Zend_Rest/Client/Zend_Rest_Client.html`.

Let us see how we can use this class to consume the Hello World service that we implemented in the previous section.

```php
<?php
require_once 'Zend/Rest/Client.php';

$client = new Zend_Rest_Client('http://localhost');

$options['method'] = 'sayHello';

$response = $client->restGet('/rest/06/hello.php', $options);

echo htmlspecialchars($response->getBody());

?>
```

We require the `client` class for this sample.

```php
require_once 'Zend/Rest/Client.php';
```

And we create the client object instance with the service host information.

```php
$client = new Zend_Rest_Client('http://localhost');
```

The request URL for the Hello service should include the name of the method we would like to invoke. As an example, for the Hello World service, the request URL would look like `http://localhost/rest/06/hello.php?method=sayHello`.

This means that the Zend REST server class expects the name of the method to be given as a request parameter in the request. Hence we use an `options` array to set this. The `array index method` is mandatory. We cannot use any other index name other than `method` to specify the method being invoked.

```php
$options['method'] = 'sayHello';
```

Next, we tell the client to send a GET request to the server proving the resource path and the request parameters.

```php
$response = $client->restGet('/rest/06/hello.php', $options);
```

We get this response and echo it as the output.

```php
echo htmlspecialchars($response->getBody());
```

And the output would look like:

```xml
<?xml version="1.0" encoding="UTF-8"?>
<sayHello generator="zend" version="1.0">
    <response>Hello World</response>
    <status>success</status>
</sayHello>
```

Library System with Zend REST classes

Now that we are familiar with the basic principles related to the REST classes that come with Zend Framework, let's explore how we can implement the library system that we used in the last two chapters as our example REST style system.

Library Service

As we saw in the last two chapters, Chapter 4 – Resource Oriented Services and Chapter 5 – Resource Oriented Clients, we need to be able to map the resource URL locations and the HTTP verbs to implement the various business operations in the library system.

Since we need to know the HTTP method being used, while implementing service operations we cannot implement the library service using the `Zend_Rest_Server` class alone with Zend Framework. This is because, by design, there is no support in the REST server class to detect the HTTP method used by the client request. As we saw in Chapter 4, the HTTP verb being used while sending a request to the service to invoke an operation determines the nature of the business operation semantics. As an example, a GET request would result in the return of currently available data and a POST request would result in the creation or update of data. In other words, GET requests would access data while POST requests would update the data. Hence, while programming services, we need to access information regarding the HTTP verb being used.

If we are to check for the `client request HTTP` method, we need to make use of `Zend_Contoller_Request_Http` class (`http://framework.zend.com/apidoc/ core/Zend_Controller/Request/Zend_Controller_Request_Http.html`). To use this class, we need to use the Model-View-Controller (MVC) constructs that come with Zend Framework. See `http://framework.zend.com/manual/en/zend. controller.html` for more details on Zend_Controller and MVC model.

The Model on MVC refers to the real-world representation of the business domain. For example, in the library system, books, members and borrowings consist of the model.

The View refers to the ways that the data being managed are viewed. For example, we may have a view to see members who have borrowed books. We would also be interested in seeing which books have been borrowed by which member in that view.

The Controller refers to the actions that the system can perform. Controller operates on the Model and performs various actions. For example, we would add a new member or create a new book borrowing.

While designing RESTful services, we map resources identified by a URI to HTTP verbs to define business operations. Resources can be thought of to represent the Model. Since HTTP verbs define the actions on the resources, the HTTP verbs to resource mapping can be thought of as Controller.

RESTful clients use HTTP verbs against resource URIs to invoke business operations. So they too use Model and Controller aspects of MVC.

Hence, REST clients and services deal with Model and Controller for the most part. While designing a Web application using REST clients to consume services, we would incorporate a View to present the data to the user. It is quite similar to the way we would use tables and forms to view and update data in a database driven application. We would connect to the database, pull data, and display that to the user with a View. We would also let the user fill forms with a View and update the database using those data filled into the forms. Likewise, when using REST services, we would request the information from a service using a REST client, and display them in a View with tables, or we will request the service to invoke an update operation using a REST client with data from forms in a View.

Because it is vital to get to know the HTTP verb in use on the server side while implementing business operations for services, we need to know how to access the information regarding the HTTP verb being used in the client request. With the request class that we get with the Zend_Controller, we have the following methods to check for the kind of request sent by the client.

- `isGet()`
- `isPost()`
- `isPut()`
- `isDelete()`
- `isHead()`

Because of this, we will be using the Zend_Controller model to implement our sample library service. And for this, we need a folder structure similar to the following.

```
library
├──application
│   ├──controllers
│   ├──layouts
│   ├──models
│   └──views
│       ├──filters
│       ├──helpers
│       └──scripts
│           └──index
└──public
```

Since we are implementing a service, we would not require the `views` folder, as there are no views or in other words, display elements or HTML pages, associated with a service.

Controllers for Book and Member Resources

The `controllers` folder contains the controllers, those PHP scripts that are responsible for handling the request for a resource. As per our sample, there would be two main resources in our library service: book and member. Hence we need two controllers.

- `BookController.php`
- `MemberController.php`

Note that having Controller suffixing the resource name is a convention that needs to be adhered to while using Zend_Controller interface.

Before looking into the controller implementations, let's first look into the models used by the controllers.

Models for Book and Member Resources

The models folder contains the data mappings for the resources. They map to the database elements that we are going to use in the library system. Again we have two main data models which are placed in the models sub-folder in our system. As explained earlier, the resources in the REST service design can be mapped to the Model in MVC.

- `books.php`
- `members.php`

The following code shows the model for book.

```php
<?php
class Books extends Zend_Db_Table
{
    protected $_name = 'book';
}
?>
```

Note how much simpler it is to use the Zend framework to work with a database. We are extending our data model for book table from the `Zend_Db_Table`. And the Zend Framework would use **PHP Data Objects (PDO)** for mapping the class into a database table. See `http://www.php.net/pdo` for more details on PDO. Basically, we do not have to deal with any SQL directly with this model.

With

```
protected $_name = 'book';
```

We specify that we want the database table named book to be mapped to Books class.

Similarly, we have the Members PHP class that maps to the members model.

```php
<?php
class Members extends Zend_Db_Table
{
    protected $_name = 'member';
}
?>
```

Note that, we did not provide any database related information in any of these classes. For providing database configuration information we can use a configuration file. The Zend_Db_Table class is capable of picking up the table column information from the database automatically; hence we need not specify the database table column names explicitly. Based on the table name assigned to the $_name attribute of the PHP class, the Zend_Db_Table class would extract the column names from the database.

Application Configuration and Initialization

We can use a configuration file with various parameters like the database name and username/password for the database. Let us name this file config.ini. We can name this file using any name that we prefer because we can tell the application what the name of the configuration is. We will see how to do this later in this section.

Here are the contents of this file.

```
[general]
db.adapter = PDO_MYSQL
db.params.host = localhost
db.params.username = sam
db.params.password = pass
db.params.dbname = library
```

This configuration is loaded by the `index.php` file, which would be located in the public folder. In addition to loading the configuration, this script also would do the other required initializations.

```php
<?php
error_reporting(E_ALL|E_STRICT);
ini_set('display_errors', 1);
date_default_timezone_set('Europe/London');

// directory setup and class loading
set_include_path('.' . PATH_SEPARATOR . '../library/'
    . PATH_SEPARATOR . '../application/models'
    . PATH_SEPARATOR . get_include_path());
include "Zend/Loader.php";
Zend_Loader::registerAutoload();

// load configuration
$config = new Zend_Config_Ini('../application/config.ini', 'general');
$registry = Zend_Registry::getInstance();
$registry->set('config', $config);

// setup database
$db = Zend_Db::factory($config->db);
Zend_Db_Table::setDefaultAdapter($db);

// setup controller
$frontController = Zend_Controller_Front::getInstance();
$frontController->throwExceptions(true);
$frontController->setControllerDirectory('../application/
controllers');
Zend_Layout::startMvc(array('layoutPath'=>'../application/layouts'));

// run!
$frontController->dispatch();
?>
```

If you follow the comments in the above code in the directory setup and class loading section, we add the models folder to the include path.

```php
set_include_path('.' . PATH_SEPARATOR . '../library/'
    . PATH_SEPARATOR . '../application/models'
    . PATH_SEPARATOR . get_include_path());
```

This step is required because we need the PHP scripts that implement models to be on the `include` path. For example, `books.php` and `members.php` must be in the `include` path because we will be using those classes while implementing business operations.

In the load configuration section we load the `config.ini` file and set it to the `Zend_Registry` instance.

```
$config = new Zend_Config_Ini('../application/config.ini', 'general');
$registry = Zend_Registry::getInstance();
$registry->set('config', $config);
```

As mentioned earlier, we could have named the configuration file with whatever name that we desire and used that name as a parameter to the `Zend_Config_Ini()` call.

Then in the setup database section, we use the database settings loaded from the configuration file to set up database parameters.

```
$db = Zend_Db::factory($config->db);
Zend_Db_Table::setDefaultAdapter($db);
```

Next, in the setup controller section, we set up the `controllers` folder.

```
$frontController = Zend_Controller_Front::getInstance();
$frontController->throwExceptions(true);
$frontController->setControllerDirectory('../application/
controllers');
```

Finally, in the run section, we dispatch the front controller instructing it to handle the incoming requests.

```
$frontController->dispatch();
```

Book Controller

Book controller implements the functionality related to the book resource. As we saw in last chapters, a GET request for the book URL would return the list of books and a POST request would create new books using the posted data.

A `controller` class needs to inherit from `Zend_Controller_Action` class.

```
class BookController extends Zend_Controller_Action {
```

Then we need to map actions to the request URL. We could map the book resource to the following URL of the application, `http://localhost/rest/06/library/public/index.php/book`.

Action mapping is done by implementing a function with the function name having the action name suffixed by `Action`.

```
function indexAction() {
```

We would use the book model within this action implementation because we are dealing with the book resource here.

```
$books = new Books();
```

We also need to make sure that the responses from this controller are not rendered as HTML, because we are implementing a service whose output is XML. Hence we disable rendering in the index action function.

```
$this->_helper->viewRenderer->setNoRender();
```

Next, we need to get to know the request method to distinguish between GET and POST requests.

```
if ($this->_request->isGet()) {
```

Check if it is a GET request.

```
} else
    if ($this->_request->isPost()) {
```

Or if it is a POST request.

In case of GET requests, we use a Zend_Rest_Server instance to deal with the request.

```
if ($this->_request->isGet()) {
    $server = new Zend_Rest_Server();
    $server->addFunction('getBooks');
    $params['method'] = 'getBooks';
    $params['book_list'] = $books->fetchAll();
    $server->handle($params);
}
```

We add a function named getBooks to the REST server.

We also need to set the parameters to be passed to the getBooks function. We use an array named params to prepare the request parameters to the REST server instance. The first parameter is the method name as required by the Zend_Rest_Server class.

```
$params['method'] = 'getBooks';
```

The client request is received by the book controller of the service. From the controller, once we get to know that it is a GET request, we map the request to the getBooks method.

The other parameter is the list of books fetched from the database.

```
$params['book_list'] = $books->fetchAll();
```

The parameter name `book_list` is the same name as the parameter name used in the `getBooks` PHP function. It is a convention used by the Zend Framework to ensure that the controller passes the correct parameters while making the function call.

Note that, because we inherited the `Books` class from `Zend_Db_Table`, we inherit the `fetchAll()` member function that we are using here to fetch data.

And then we call the `handle` method of the REST server instance with the parameters.

```
$server->handle($params);
```

This call would basically call the `getBooks` function with the `book_list` parameter.

The `getBooks` function formulates the XML response from the list of books. This function will be defined in the same PHP script where we define the book controller.

```php
function getBooks($book_list) {
    $result = '<?xml version="1.0" encoding="UTF-8"?><books>';
    foreach ($book_list as $book) {
        $result .= "<book><id>" . $book->id . "</id>" .
        "<name>" . $book->name . "</name>" .
        "<author>" . $book->author . "</author>" .
        "<isbn>" . $book->isbn . "</isbn></book>";
    }
    $result .= "</books>";
    $xml = simplexml_load_string($result);
    return $xml;
}
```

This function traverses through the list of books using a `foreach` loop and forms the XML response to be returned as response.

That is how the book controller is handling the GET requests.

In case of POST requests, we load the incoming XML request data posted and create new book instances in the database.

```php
if ($this->_request->isPost()) {
    $xml = simplexml_load_string($this->_request-
                                >getRawBody());
    foreach ($xml->book as $book) {
        $row = $books->createRow();
        $row->name = $book->name;
        $row->author = $book->author;
        $row->isbn = $book->isbn;
        $row->save();
    }
}
```

First, the raw XML data in the POST request body is loaded as a simple XML object instance.

```
$xml = simplexml_load_string($this->_request->getRawBody());
```

Then for each book element in the XML payload,

```
foreach ($xml->book as $book) {
```

We create a new database table row in the book table,

```
$row = $books->createRow();
```

Assign the values received in the request corresponding to the new book instance,

```
$row->name = $book->name;
$row->author = $book->author;
$row->isbn = $book->isbn;
```

And save the newly created database row.

```
$row->save();
```

Note that we are not using an instance of a Zend_Rest_Server in case of a POST request. Because we are not returning any response in case of a POST request and also because we could use an instance of a Books class, the book model, to deal with the database operations, use of a REST server instance would be an overkill here. If the request succeeds, the server would be sending a 200 OK response. If the request fails, the server would send some error status code, such as 500 Internal server error. This would be handled by the framework. The client can get to know the success or failure by tracking the HTTP status code.

Here is an example response for the success case.

```
HTTP/1.1 200 OK
Date: Sun, 14 Sep 2008 14:35:57 GMT
Server: Apache/2.2.6 (Win32) mod_ssl/2.2.6 OpenSSL/0.9.8e PHP/5.2.5
X-Powered-By: PHP/5.2.5
Content-Length: 0
Content-Type: text/html
```

Here is the complete code for the PHP script implementing the book controller.

```php
<?php
require_once 'Zend/Rest/Server.php';

function getBooks($book_list) {
    $result = '<?xml version="1.0" encoding="UTF-8"?><books>';
    foreach ($book_list as $book) {
```

```
            $result .= "<book><id>" . $book->id . "</id>" .
            "<name>" . $book->name . "</name>" .
            "<author>" . $book->author . "</author>" .
            "<isbn>" . $book->isbn . "</isbn></book>";
        }
        $result .= "</books>";
        $xml = simplexml_load_string($result);
        return $xml;
    }

    class BookController extends Zend_Controller_Action {
        function indexAction() {
            $books = new Books();
            $this->_helper->viewRenderer->setNoRender();

            if ($this->_request->isGet()) {
                $server = new Zend_Rest_Server();
                $server->addFunction('getBooks');
                $params['method'] = 'getBooks';
                $params['book_list'] = $books->fetchAll();
                $server->handle($params);
            } else
                if ($this->_request->isPost()) {
                    $xml = simplexml_load_string($this->_request-
                                                >getRawBody());
                    foreach ($xml->book as $book) {
                        $row = $books->createRow();
                        $row->name = $book->name;
                        $row->author = $book->author;
                        $row->isbn = $book->isbn;
                        $row->save();
                    }
                }
        }
    }
?>
```

Member Controller

The implementation of the member controller class to represent the member resource is very similar to the book controller, except for a few differences.

First we could map the member resource to the following URL of the application, http://localhost/rest/06/library/public/index.php/member.

```
    class MemberController extends Zend_Controller_Action {
```

And we use the member data model in the index action function.

```
function indexAction() {
    $members = new Members();
    $this->_helper->viewRenderer->setNoRender();
```

If it is a GET request, we call the get members function.

```
    if ($this->_request->isGet()) {
        $server = new Zend_Rest_Server();
        $server->addFunction('getMembers');
        $params['method'] = 'getMembers';
        $params['member_list'] = $members->fetchAll();
        $server->handle($params);
    }
```

And here is the function added to the service.

```
function getMembers($member_list) {
    $members = array ();
    $result = '<?xml version="1.0" encoding="UTF-8"?><members>';
    foreach ($member_list as $member) {
        $result .= "<member><id>" . $member->id . "</id>" .
        "<first_name>" . $member->first_name . "</first_name>" .
        "<last_name>" . $member->last_name . "</last_name></member>";
    }
    $result .= "</members>";
    $xml = simplexml_load_string($result);
    return $xml;
}
```

And in case of a POST request, we create new member instances.

```
        if ($this->_request->isPost()) {
            $xml = simplexml_load_string($this->_request-
>getRawBody());
            foreach ($xml->member as $member) {
                $row = $members->createRow();
                $row->first_name = $member->first_name;
                $row->last_name = $member->last_name;
                $row->save();
            }
        }
```

Here is the complete source code for the member controller PHP class.

```php
<?php
require_once 'Zend/Rest/Server.php';

function getMembers($member_list) {
    $members = array ();
    $result = '<?xml version="1.0" encoding="UTF-8"?><members>';
    foreach ($member_list as $member) {
        $result .= "<member><id>" . $member->id . "</id>" .
        "<first_name>" . $member->first_name . "</first_name>" .
        "<last_name>" . $member->last_name . "</last_name></member>";
    }
    $result .= "</members>";

    $xml = simplexml_load_string($result);
    return $xml;
}

class MemberController extends Zend_Controller_Action {
    function indexAction() {
        $members = new Members();
        $this->_helper->viewRenderer->setNoRender();

        if ($this->_request->isGet()) {
            $server = new Zend_Rest_Server();
            $server->addFunction('getMembers');
            $params['method'] = 'getMembers';
            $params['member_list'] = $members->fetchAll();
            $server->handle($params);
        } else
            if ($this->_request->isPost()) {
                $xml = simplexml_load_string($this->_request-
                                    >getRawBody());
                foreach ($xml->member as $member) {
                    $row = $members->createRow();
                    $row->first_name = $member->first_name;
                    $row->last_name = $member->last_name;
                    $row->save();
                }
            }
    }
}
?>
```

Library Clients

The previous section explained how to implement the service resources. Now let's consume those services using `Zend_Rest_Client` class. Again, we can use the `Zend_Controller` to leverage the MVC model. Since the client would be using views, we are better off using an MVC.

Again, for the client application we need a folder structure similar to the following.

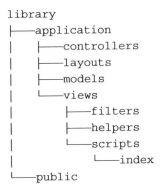

```
library
├──application
│   ├──controllers
│   ├──layouts
│   ├──models
│   └──views
│       ├──filters
│       ├──helpers
│       └──scripts
│           └──index
└──public
```

Again we will require a controller for the client application, but unlike in the case of service, we will not use the controller class to map to a resource. We will use it as an entry point of the client application. The client application is a Web application. It should handle the requests from the users and provide the users with views. The controller of the client application would take care of this.

```
class IndexController extends Zend_Controller_Action {
```

List Books with GET

We will map the index action of `IndexController` to the request that displays the list of books.

```
function indexAction() {
    $this->view->title = "Books";
    $client = new Zend_Rest_Client('http://localhost');
    $response = $client->restGet('/rest/06/library/public/index.
php/book');
    $this->view->books = simplexml_load_string($response-
                                            >getBody());

}
```

We are using a `Zend_Rest_Client` instance to access the service. We send a GET request to the book resource.

```
$client = new Zend_Rest_Client('http://localhost');
$response = $client->restGet('/rest/06/library/public/index.
php/book');
```

We are expecting an XML document as the response for the GET request. We load the request body as a simple XML object instance and assign that to the books member of the view.

```
$this->view->books = simplexml_load_string($response->getBody());
```

The template for the book view is located in the `library\application\views\scripts\index` sub folder. Since we are using the index action for listing books, the template for the view must be placed in a file named `index.phtml`. This is an MVC related convention used by the Zend Framework.

Here is the template for books view.

```
<h2>List of Books</h2>
<table>
<tr>
    <th>Name</th>
    <th>Author</th>
    <th>ISBN</th>
</tr>
<?php foreach($this->books->book as $book) : ?>
<tr>
    <td><?php echo $this->escape($book->name);?></td>
    <td><?php echo $this->escape($book->author);?></td>
    <td><?php echo $this->escape($book->isbn);?></td>
</tr>
<?php endforeach; ?>
</table>

<p><a href="<?php echo $this->url(array('controller'=>'index',
    'action'=>'addBook'));?>">Add new book</a></p>
```

In the view, we loop through each book in the books XML structure that was passed on to the view from the controller and display all the book information in a table.

```
<?php foreach($this->books->book as $book) : ?>
<tr>
    <td><?php echo $this->escape($book->name);?></td>
    <td><?php echo $this->escape($book->author);?></td>
    <td><?php echo $this->escape($book->isbn);?></td>
</tr>
<?php endforeach; ?>
```

And at the end of the page we display a link that would lead to a form that can be used to add a book.

When you access the client application's index URL, `http://localhost/rest/06/library/public/index.php/index` with the Web browser, you will see an output similar to the following.

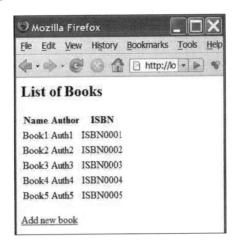

Add a Book with POST

Next, adding a book. For this, we add a new action `addbook`.

```
function addbookAction() {
```

When this action is requested by the user, by clicking on the Add new book link, as shown in the earlier screenshot, we display a form to the user and get the data for a new book.

```
$form = new BookForm();
$form->submit->setLabel('Add');
$this->view->form = $form;
```

This will make sure that the book form would be displayed to the user. We use an instance of `BookForm` model to capture the data. The model script, `bookForm.php` is placed in the models sub-folder. `BookForm` class is inherited from `Zend_Form` class. And we capture the name, author and ISBN data for the new book using this form. Here is the PHP code for the `BookForm` model.

```php
<?php

class BookForm extends Zend_Form
{
    public function __construct($options = null)
```

```
        {
                parent::__construct($options);
                $this->setName('book');

                $name = new Zend_Form_Element_Text('name');
                $name->setLabel('Name')
                ->setRequired(true)
                ->addFilter('StripTags')
                ->addFilter('StringTrim')
                ->addValidator('NotEmpty');

                $author = new Zend_Form_Element_Text('author');
                $author->setLabel('Author')
                ->setRequired(true)
                ->addFilter('StripTags')
                ->addFilter('StringTrim')
                ->addValidator('NotEmpty');

                  $isbn = new Zend_Form_Element_Text('isbn');
                $isbn->setLabel('ISBN')
                ->setRequired(true)
                ->addFilter('StripTags')
                ->addFilter('StringTrim')
                ->addValidator('NotEmpty');

                $id = new Zend_Form_Element_Hidden('id');

                $submit = new Zend_Form_Element_Submit('submit');
                $submit->setAttrib('id', 'submitbutton');

                $this->addElements(array($id, $name, $author, $isbn,
    $submit));
        }
}
?>
```

We have three text form elements and a **Submit** button added to this form. The advantage of using Zend_Form here is that the data submitted would be accessible using simple methods in the controller. For the user, this form would be rendered through the view for the user to submit the data.

The view template corresponding to the action addbook would be named add-book.phtml and would be placed in library\application\views\scripts \index folder. And the view template is very simple. All that you have to do is to render the form.

```
<?php echo $this->form ;?>
```

This will look on the browser like the following.

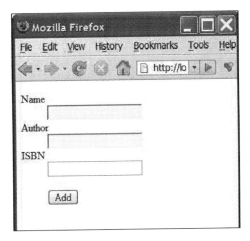

Next, in the `addbookAction` function, we check if the request is a POST request.

```
if ($this->_request->isPost()) {
    $formData = $this->_request->getPost();
    if ($form->isValid($formData)) {
        $client = new Zend_Rest_Client('http://localhost');

        $request = '<?xml version="1.0" encoding="UTF-
                    8"?><books>';
        $request .= "<book><name>" . $form->getValue('name') .
                    "</name>" .
        "<author>" . $form->getValue('author') . "</author>" .
        "<isbn>" . $form->getValue('isbn') . "</isbn></book>";
        $request .= "</books>";

        $response = $client->restPost('/rest/06/library/
public/index.php/book', $request);
        $this->_redirect('/');
    }
}
```

If the request is a POST, we access the form data posted.

```
$formData = $this->_request->getPost();
```

And we create a `Zend_Rest_Client` instance.

```
$client = new Zend_Rest_Client('http://localhost');
```

Prepare the XML to be posted to the book resource URL.

```
$request = '<?xml version="1.0" encoding="UTF-
                8"?><books>';
$request .= "<book><name>" . $form->getValue('name') .
                "</name>" .
"<author>" . $form->getValue('author') . "</author>" .
"<isbn>" . $form->getValue('isbn') . "</isbn></book>";
$request .= "</books>";
```

And we post that data to the book resource URL to create a new book.

```
$response = $client->restPost(
    '/rest/06/library/public/index.php/book', $request);
```

Here is the complete code for the add book action.

```
function addbookAction() {
    $this->view->title = "Add New Book";
    $form = new BookForm();
    $form->submit->setLabel('Add');
    $this->view->form = $form;
    if ($this->_request->isPost()) {
        $formData = $this->_request->getPost();
        if ($form->isValid($formData)) {
            $client = new Zend_Rest_Client('http://localhost');
            $request = '<?xml version="1.0" encoding="UTF
                -8"?><books>';
            $request .= "<book><name>" . $form->getValue('name') .
                "</name>" .
            "<author>" . $form->getValue('author') . "</author>" .
            "<isbn>" . $form->getValue('isbn') . "</isbn></book>";
            $request .= "</books>";
            $response = $client->restPost('/rest/06/library/
public/index.php/book', $request);
            $this->_redirect('/');
        }
    }
}
```

List Members with GET

Listing members is quite similar to listing books.

We map the member listing URL to http://localhost/rest/06/library/public/index.php/index/members. This means that we need an action named members on the client application.

Here is the `action` function.

```
function membersAction() {
    $this->view->title = "Members";
    $client = new Zend_Rest_Client('http://localhost');
    $response = $client->restGet('/rest/06/library/public/index.
php/member');

    $this->view->members = simplexml_load_string($response-
                                                 >getBody());

}
```

And the view template is as follows:

```
<h2>List of Members</h2>
<table>
<tr>
    <th>First Name</th>
    <th>Last Name</th>
</tr>
<?php foreach($this->members->member as $member) : ?>
<tr>
    <td><?php echo $this->escape($member->first_name);?></td>
    <td><?php echo $this->escape($member->last_name);?></td>
</tr>
<?php endforeach; ?>
</table>
<p><a href="<?php echo $this->url(array('controller'=>'index',
        'action'=>'addMember'));?>">Add new member</a></p>
```

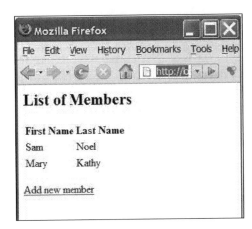

The above screenshot shows how the member listing looks when accessed with the browser.

Add a Member with POST

We would map the add member operation of the client application to the addMember action.

```php
function addMember() {
    $this->view->title = "Add New Member";

    $form = new MemberForm();
    $form->submit->setLabel('Add');
    $this->view->form = $form;

    if ($this->_request->isPost()) {
        $formData = $this->_request->getPost();
        if ($form->isValid($formData)) {
            $client = new Zend_Rest_Client('http://localhost');

            $request = '<?xml version="1.0" encoding="UTF-
                        8"?><members>';
            $request .= "<member><first_name>" . $form-
>getValue('first_name') . "</first_name>" .
                        "<last_name>" . $form->getValue('last_name') . "</
last_name></member>";
            $request .= "</members>";

            $xml = simplexml_load_string($request);

            $response = $client->restPost('/rest/06/library/
public/index.php/member', $request);
            $this->_redirect('/index/members');
        }
    }
}
```

This action is similar to that of the book add operation, but we use a MemberForm model here.

Here is the member form to capture first name and last name of the new member.

```php
<?php

class MemberForm extends Zend_Form
{
    public function __construct($options = null)
    {
        parent::__construct($options);
        $this->setName('member');

        $name = new Zend_Form_Element_Text('first_name');
        $name->setLabel('First Name')
        ->setRequired(true)
        ->addFilter('StripTags')
```

```
        ->addFilter('StringTrim')
        ->addValidator('NotEmpty');
    $author = new Zend_Form_Element_Text('last_name');
    $author->setLabel('Last Name')
        ->setRequired(true)
        ->addFilter('StripTags')
        ->addFilter('StringTrim')
        ->addValidator('NotEmpty');
    $id = new Zend_Form_Element_Hidden('id');
    $submit = new Zend_Form_Element_Submit('submit');
    $submit->setAttrib('id', 'submitbutton');
    $this->addElements(array($id, $name, $author, $submit));
    }
}
?>
```

And this is rendered through `add-member.phtml` view template.

```
<?php echo $this->form ;?>
```

And it would look like the following with the Web browser.

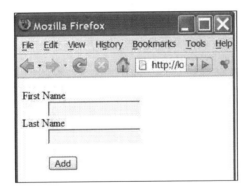

Complete Client Application Controller

As we discussed in the above sections, client application supports adding and viewing book and member information. Here is the complete PHP source code for the client controller.

```php
<?php
require_once 'Zend/Rest/Client.php';
class IndexController extends Zend_Controller_Action {
    function indexAction() {
        $this->view->title = "Books";
```

```php
        $client = new Zend_Rest_Client('http://localhost');
        $response = $client->restGet('/rest/06/library/public/index.
php/book');

        $this->view->books = simplexml_load_string($response-
>getBody());
    }

    function addbookAction() {
        $this->view->title = "Add New Book";

        $form = new BookForm();
        $form->submit->setLabel('Add');
        $this->view->form = $form;

        if ($this->_request->isPost()) {
            $formData = $this->_request->getPost();
            if ($form->isValid($formData)) {
                $client = new Zend_Rest_Client('http://localhost');

                $request = '<?xml version="1.0" encoding="UTF-
                            8"?><books>';
                $request .= "<book><name>" . $form->getValue('name') .
                            "</name>" .
                "<author>" . $form->getValue('author') . "</author>" .
                "<isbn>" . $form->getValue('isbn') . "</isbn></book>";
                $request .= "</books>";

                $response = $client-
                >restPost('/rest/06/library/public/index.php/book',
$request);

                $this->_redirect('/');
            }
        }
    }

    function membersAction() {
        $this->view->title = "Members";
        $client = new Zend_Rest_Client('http://localhost');
        $response = $client-
                    >restGet('/rest/06/library/public/index.php/
member');

        $this->view->members = simplexml_load_string($response-
                                                    >getBody());
    }

    function addMember() {
        $this->view->title = "Add New Member";

        $form = new MemberForm();
```

```
        $form->submit->setLabel('Add');
        $this->view->form = $form;

    if ($this->_request->isPost()) {
            $formData = $this->_request->getPost();
            if ($form->isValid($formData)) {
                $client = new Zend_Rest_Client('http://localhost');

                $request = '<?xml version="1.0" encoding="UTF-
                            8"?><members>';
                $request .= "<member><first_name>" . $form-
    >getValue('first_name') . "</first_name>" .
                    "<last_name>" . $form->getValue('last_name') . "</
    last_name></member>";
                $request .= "</members>";

                $xml = simplexml_load_string($request);

                $response = $client->restPost('/rest/06/library/
    public/index.php/member', $request);
                $this->_redirect('/index/members');
            }
        }
    }
}
?>
```

Summary

In this chapter, we used the REST classes provided with the Zend Framework to implement the sample library system. The design of the service and client was covered along with the MVC concepts supported by the Zend Framework.

We discussed how resources map to the Model in MVC. Then we also discussed how HTTP verbs, when combined with resource URIs, map to the Controller in MVC.

We discussed how to combine Zend_Rest_Server with Zend_Controller to implement the business operations of the service.

We also explored how to use Zend_Rest_Client class to consume the services. And we implemented a sample web-based application using REST client to consume the REST service.

In the next chapter, we will discuss how to debug and troubleshoot REST services and clients.

7
Debugging REST Web Services

Learning how to figure out why things are going wrong is one of the key aspects of developing software. We call it debugging. While dealing with REST services and clients, things can go wrong and it would help a great deal to know how to find out what is causing the problems.

In this chapter, we will look into the techniques such as message capturing and analysing to get to know if things are going fine, and if not, what sort of problems are causing trouble.

Message Tracing

The first symptom that you will notice when you are running into problems is that the client would not behave the way you want it to behave. As an example, there would be no output, or the wrong output.

Since the outcome of running a REST client depends on the request that you send over the wire and the response that you receive over the wire, one of the first things is to capture the messages and verify that those are in the correct expected format.

REST Services and clients interact using messages, usually in pairs of request and response. So if there are problems, they are caused by errors in the messages being exchanged.

Sometimes the user only has control over a REST client and does not have access to the implementation details of the service. Sometimes the user will implement the REST service for others to consume the service. Sometimes the Web browser can act as a client. Sometimes a PHP application on a server can act as a REST client. Irrespective of where the client is and where the service is, you can use message capturing tools to capture messages and try to figure out the problem. Thanks to the fact that the service and client use messages to interact with each other, we can always use a message capturing tool in the middle to capture messages. It is not that we must run the message capturing tool on the same machine where the client is running or the service is running; the message capturing tool can be run on either machine, or it can be run on a third machine.

The following figure illustrates how the message interaction would look with a message capturing tool in place.

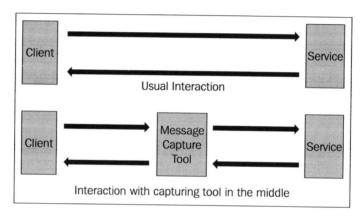

If the REST client is a Web browser and we want to capture the request and response involved in a message interaction, we would have to point the Web browser to message capturing tool and let the tool send the request to the service on behalf of the Web browser. Then, since it is the tool that sent the request to the service, the service would respond to the tool. The message capturing tool in turn would send the response it received from the service to the Web browser. In this scenario, the tool in the middle would gain access to both the request and response. Hence it can reveal those messages for us to have a look.

When you are not seeing the client to work, here is the list of things that you might need to look for:

- If the client sends a message
- If you are able to receive a response from a service
- If the request message sent by the client is in the correct format, including HTTP headers
- If the response sent by the server is in the correct format, including the HTTP headers

In order to check for the above, you would require a message-capturing tool to trace the messages.

There are multiple tools that you can use to capture the messages that are sent from the client to the service and vice versa. Wireshark (`http://www.wireshark.org/`) is one such tool that can be used to capture any network traffic. It is an open-source tool and is available under the GNU General Public License version 2. However this tool can be a bit complicated if you are looking for a simple tool.

Apache TCPMon (`http://ws.apache.org/commons/tcpmon/`) is another tool that is designed to trace web services messages. This is a Java based tool that can be used with web services to capture the messages. Because TCPMon is a message capturing tool, it can be used to intercept messages sent between client and service, and as explained earlier, can be run on the client machine, the server machine or on a third independent machine. The only catch is that you need Java installed in your system to run this tool. You can also find a C-based implementation of a similar tool with Apache Axis2/C (`http://ws.apache.org/axis2/c`). However, that tool does not have a graphical user interface.

There is a set of steps that you need to follow, which are more or less the same across all of these tools, in order to prepare the tool for capturing messages.

- Define the target host name
- Define the target port number
- Define the listen port number

Target host name is the name of the host machine on which the service is running. As an example, if we want to debug the request sent to the Yahoo spelling suggestion service, hosted at `http://search.yahooapis.com/WebSearchService/V1/spellingSuggestion`, the host name would be `search.yahooapis.com`. We can either use the name of the host or we can use the IP address of the host because the tools are capable of dealing with both formats in place of the host name. As an example, if the service is hosted on the local machine, we could either use `localhost` or `127.0.0.1` in place of the host name.

Target port number is the port number on which the service hosting web server is listening; usually this is 80. As an example, for the Yahoo spelling suggestion service, hosted at `http://search.yahooapis.com/WebSearchService/V1/spellingSuggestion`, the target port number is 80. Note that, when the service URL does not mention any number, we can always use the default number. If it was running on a port other than port 80, we can find the port number followed by the host name and preceded with caracter ':'. As an example, if we have our web server running on port 8080 on the local machine, we would have service URL similar to `http://localhost:8080/rest/04/library/book.php`. Here, the host name is `localhost` and the target port is 8080.

Listen port is the port on which the tool will be listening to capture the messages from the client before sending it to the service. For an example, say that we want to use port 9090 as our listen port to capture the messages while using the Yahoo spelling suggestion service. Under normal circumstances, we will be using a URL similar to the following with the web browser to send the request to the service.

```
http://search.yahooapis.com/WebSearchService/V1/spellingSuggestion
    ?appid=YahooDemo&query=apocalipto
```

When we want to send this request through the message capturing tool and since we decided to make the tools listen port to be 9090 with the tool in the middle and assuming that the tool is running on the local machine, we would now use the following URL with the web browser in place of the original URL.

```
http://localhost:9090/WebSearchService/V1/spellingSuggestion?appid
    =YahooDemo&query=apocalipto
```

Note that we are not sending this request directly to `search.yahooapis.com`, but rather to the tool listening on port 9090 on local host. Once the tool receives the request, it will capture the request, forward that to the target host, receive the response and forward that response to the web browser.

The following figure shows the Apache TCPMon tool. You can see localhost being used as the target host, 80 being the target port number and 9090 being the listening port number. Once you fill in these fields you can see a new tab being added in the tool showing the messages being captured.

Once you click on the **Add** button, you will see a new pane as shown in the next figure where it will show the messages and pass the messages to and from the client and service.

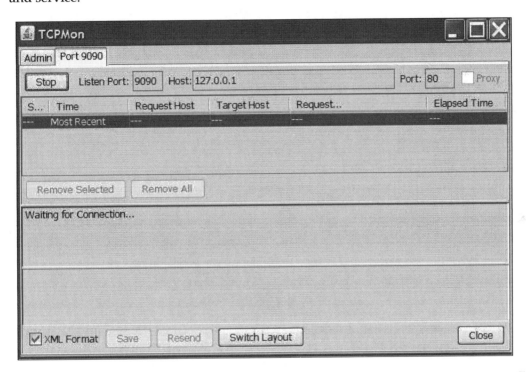

Before you can capture the messages, there is one more step. That is to change the client code to point to the port number 9090, since our monitoring tool is now listening on that port. Originally, we were using port 80.

```
$url = 'http://localhost:80/rest/04/library/book.php';
```

or just

```
$url = 'http://localhost/rest/04/library/book.php';
```

because the default port number used by a web server is port 80, and the client was directly talking to the service. However, with the tool in place, we are going to make the client talk to the tool listening on port 9090. The tool in turn will talk to the service. Note that in this sample we have all three parties, the client, the service, and the tool running on the same machine. So we will keep using localhost as our host name.

Now we are going to change the service endpoint address used by the client to contain port 9090. This will make sure that the client will be talking to the tool.

```
$url = 'http://localhost:9090/rest/04/library/book.php';
```

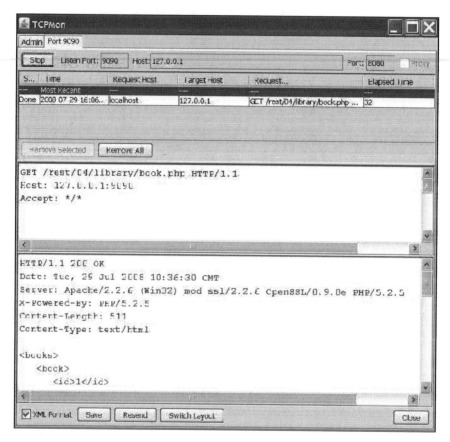

As you can see, the tool has captured the request and the response. The request appears at the top and the response at the bottom. The request is a GET request to the resource located at /rest/04/library/book.php. The response is a success response, with HTTP 200 OK code. And after the HTTP headers, the response body, which is in XML follows.

As mentioned earlier, the first step in debugging is to verify if the client has sent a request and if the service responded. In the above example, we have both the request and response in place. If both were missing then we need to check what is wrong on either side.

If the client request was missing, you can check for the following in the code.

- Are you using the correct URL in client
- Have you written the request to the wire in the client? Usually this is done by the function `curl_exec` when using Curl

If the response was missing, you can check for the following.

- Are you connected to the network? Because your service can be hosted on a remote machine
- Have you written a response from the service? That is, basically, have you returned the correct string value from the service? In PHP wire, using the echo function to write the required response to the wire usually does this. If you are using a PHP framework, you may have to use the framework specific mechanisms to do this. As an example, if you are using the `Zend_Rest_Server` class, you have to use `handle()` method to make sure that the response is sent to the client.

Here is a sample error scenario.

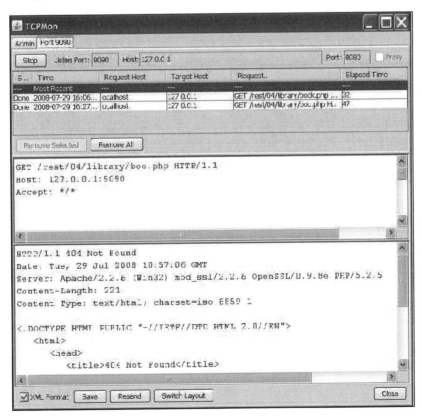

As you can see, the response is **404 not found**. And if you look at the request, you see that there is a typo in the request. We have missed 'k' from our resource URL, hence we have sent the request to `/rest/04/library/boo.php`, which does not exist, whereas the correct resource URL is `/rest/04/library/book.php`.

Next let us look at the Yahoo search example that was discussed earlier to identify some advanced concepts. We want to capture the request sent by the web browser and the response sent by the server for the request. `http://search.yahooapis.com/WebSearchService/V1/spellingSuggestion?appid=YahooDemo&query=apocalipto`.

As discussed earlier, the target host name is search.`yahooapis.com`. The target port number is 80. Let's use 9091 as the listen.

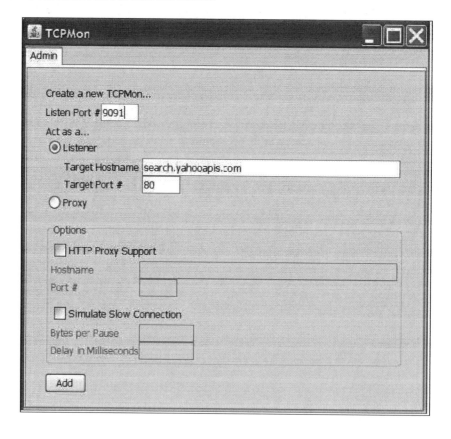

Let us use the web browser to send the request through the tool so that we can capture the request and response. Since the tool is listening on port 9091, we would use the following URL with the web browser. `http://localhost:9091/WebSearchService/V1/spellingSuggestion?appid=YahooDemo&query=apocalipto`

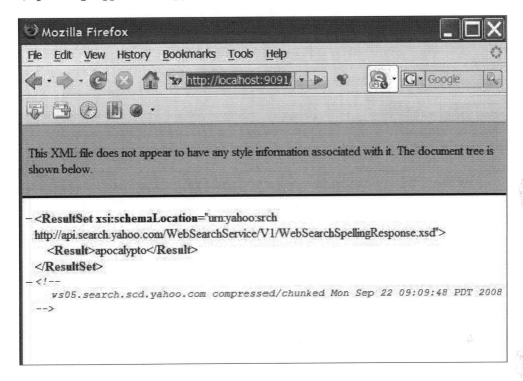

When you use the above URL with the web browser, the web browser would send the request to the tool and the tool will get the response from the service and forward that to the web browser. We can see that the web browser gets the response.

However, if we have a look at the TCPMon tool's captured messages, we see that the service has sent some binary data instead of XML data even though the Web browser is displaying the response in XML format.

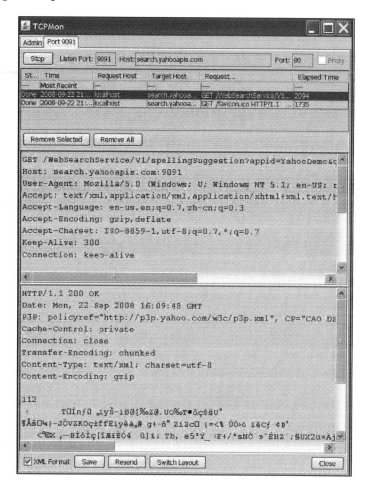

So what went wrong? In fact, nothing is wrong. The service sent the data in binary format because the web browser requested that format. If you look closely at the request sent you will see the following.

```
GET /WebSearchService/V1/spellingSuggestion?appid=YahooDemo&query=apoc
alipto HTTP/1.1
Host: search.yahooapis.com:9091
User-Agent: Mozilla/5.0 (Windows; U; Windows NT 5.1; en-US;
rv:1.8.1.9) Gecko/20071025 Firefox/2.0.0.9
Accept: text/xml,application/xml,application/xhtml+xml,text/
html;q=0.9,text/plain;q=0.8,image/png,*/*;q=0.5
Accept-Language: en-us,en;q=0.7,zh-cn;q=0.3
```

```
Accept-Encoding: gzip,deflate
Accept-Charset: ISO-8859-1,utf-8;q=0.7,*;q=0.7
Keep-Alive: 300
Connection: keep-alive
```

In the request, the web browser has used the HTTP header.

```
Accept-Encoding: gzip,deflate
```

This tells the service that the web browser can handle data that comes in gzip compressed format. Hence the service sends the data compressed to the web browser. Obviously, it is not possible to look into the XML messages and debug them if the response is compressed. Hence we should ideally capture the messages in XML format. To do this, we can modify the request message on the TCPMon pane itself and resend the message.

First remove the line

```
Accept-Encoding: gzip,deflate
```

Then click on the **Resend** button.

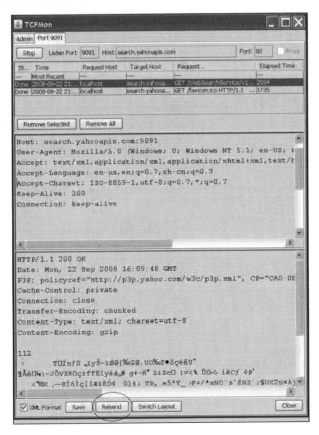

Once we click on the **Resend** button, we will get the response in XML format.

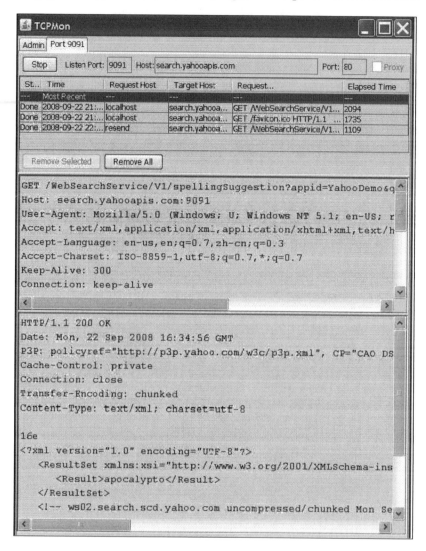

Errors in Building XML

While forming XML as request payload or response payload, we can run into errors through simple mistakes. Some would be easy to spot but some are not. Most of the XML errors could be avoided by following a simple rule of thumb-each opening XML tag should have an equivalent closing tag. That is the common mistake that can happen while building XML payloads.

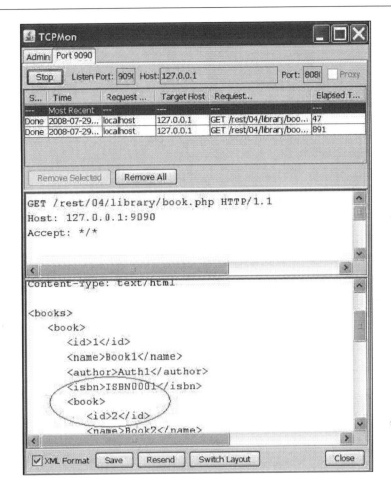

In the above diagram, if you look carefully in the circle, the ending tag for the book element is missing. A new starting tag for a new book is started before the first book is closed. This would cause the XML parsing on the client side to fail. In this case I am using the Library system sample and here is the PHP source code causing the problem.

```php
echo "<books>";
while ($line = mysql_fetch_array($result, MYSQL_ASSOC)) {
    echo "<book>";
    foreach ($line as $key => $col_value) {
        echo "<$key>$col_value</$key>";
    }
    //echo "</book>";
}
echo "</books>";
```

Here I have intentionally commented out printing the closing tag to demonstrate the error scenario. However, while writing this code, I could have missed that as well, causing the system to be buggy.

While looking for XML related errors, you can use the manual technique that we just used. Look for missing tags. If the process looks complicated and you cannot seem to find any XML errors in the response or request that you are trying to debug, you can copy the XML captured with the tool and run it through an XML validator tool. For example, you can use an online tool such as `http://www.w3schools.com/XML/xml_validator.asp`. You can also check if the XML file is well formed using an XML parser.

Errors in Parsing XML

There also can be situations where you could make mistakes while parsing an incoming XML message. As an example, have a look at the following code.

```
foreach ($xml->book as $book) {
    echo "$book->id, $book->name, $book->author, $book->isbn <br/>\n";
}
```

Here, the parsing logic assumes the following XML format.

```
<books>
    <book>
        <id>1</id>
        <name>Book1</name>
        <author>Auth1</author>
        <isbn>ISBN0001</isbn>
    </book>
</books>
```

There are two common possibilities where typos can happen while parsing an XML. First, the `foreach` statement.

```
foreach ($xml->book as $book) {
```

Here, the common mistake is to forget that the root element, `book` in this example corresponds to the `$xml` element. It is a common mistake to use

```
$xml->books->book
```

in place of

```
$xml->book
```

The second possibility is to use incorrect element names while using the child elements of a given element. In this example, we use

```
echo "$book->id, $book->name, $book->author, $book->isbn <br/>\n";
```

If we were to use

```
$book->ISBN
```

instead of

```
$book->isbn
```

The client would not behave as expected and would not print the ISBN number in the output. This is because XML is case sensitive and the incoming XML has the element name `<isbn>` and not `<ISBN>`.

Best Practices

Best practices would help us avoid common mistakes while using REST style services and clients.

- Make sure that you are using the correct HTTP method. You can trace the messages and have a look at the HTTP method used in the request. Note that the HTTP verb being used has significance in the REST operations. Therefore, it is good practice to always pay attention to the HTTP verb being used while invoking operations.

- Always verify the integrity of your XML messages, both request and response. Check for exact spelling of field key names because, as mentioned earlier, XML is case sensitive. Also check if all mandatory fields are in place. Often the service API document would clearly highlight and distinguish mandatory and optional fields. Some API documents would not mention if a field is mandatory or not. In that case you might have to assume that every field is mandatory.

- If you happen to run into problems and cannot figure out what is going wrong in case of the business logic of a service, try to run the business logic as a standalone program rather than making it a service. In other words, make sure you do comprehensive unit testing of the functionality. That will help reduce the complexity to help locate the problems easily.

- The above style of divide and conquer approach can also be applied on client side as well. As an example, if you seem to have problems with parsing the response, use a sample XML file that has the identical structure to that of response and try to test the parsing logic standalone.

- If you are using third-party services that you did not write, make sure you have access to comprehensive documentation that explains the message formats and request parameters. Especially the sample messages, which indicate what the request and response would look like, would help with debugging.

- Look for sample code segments provided to you by the service provider. Most public service APIs come with such examples.

- If you are using public services such as Google, Yahoo, etc. there are wrapper PHP classes provided by the service vendors to help you consume the services. Look for those classes, rather than writing it from scratch. The Zend framework also provides a set of such wrapper classes for some public REST services.

- If you are using a framework for your application, look for framework specific logging and debugging features. Most frameworks provide you with comprehensive logging along with the ability to customize log levels to help you locate problems.

- If you are planning on providing REST services of your own, make sure that you clearly document the service API along with all mandatory and optional fields. Most of the time, just pointing users to the documents would solve a considerable amount of problems.

- Try to avoid re-inventing the HTTP verbs mappings if you are designing services. Stick to the basic meanings of HTTP verbs that we discussed in Chapter 1. For example, use GET to retrieve data and POST for updating data. Do not use POST to retrieve data.

- Keep in mind that the client and the service are two independent entities. All the interaction between those two takes place using messages. Hence avoid making any assumptions about either party. All information that is required for the interaction must be self-contained within the messages passed between the client and the service. This interaction must be stateless, meaning that each request/response pair is executed independently without any knowledge of the request/response that happened before or that is to happen in the future. This will make sure that the client and service interaction is kept atomic, and ensure that the interactions are simple.

- While designing services, make sure the request and response message formats are kept simple. This is because, more complex the messages formats are the harder it is to debug applications. At the same time, the number of interactions between the client and the service that are required to get some effective work done must also be kept to a minimum. This is because the more interactions we need the more we will have to use the network and the latency of the network would be the governing factor that would determine our application's performance. Hence the right balance between the message size and the number of request/response interactions must be determined. The rule of thumb to follow would be to do whatever necessary, not more and not less. For example, in Chapter 5 while designing the library system, we just followed the REST principles and came up with the design. The message formats were not too complicated. Also the number of interactions just matched the requirement.

Summary

We looked into the use of tools to trace and look into the messages to figure out possible problems with request and response pairs passed between clients and services. We also looked into how we could look at the XML to figure out possible problems in building XML. We also discussed how we can locate problems in parsing an incoming XML.

A
WSO2 Web Services
Framework for PHP

WSO2 Web Services Framework for PHP (WSO2 WSF/PHP) is an open-source, enterprise grade PHP extension for providing and consuming web services in PHP. The home page for the project can be found at `http://wso2.org/projects/wsf/php`. WSO2 WSF/PHP is a complete solution for building and deploying web services and is the only PHP extension with the widest range of `WS-*` (also known as SOAP web services) specification implementations. It is also notable that it has a comprehensive REST support. You can implement a single service and expose it as both SOAP and REST service. Please refer to Chapter 1 for a recap of REST and SOAP comparison.

In Chapter 6 we introduced Zend Framework. The key difference between WSF/PHP and the Zend Framework is that, while Zend framework is a library written in PHP, WSF/PHP is a library written in C as a PHP extension. Also, while Zend Framework is a generic PHP library that also includes REST support. WSF/PHP is a web services specific framework that supports REST as well as SOAP services. You can use WSF/PHP as a REST framework alone or you can use it for SOAP web services that require quality of service aspects such as security and reliability.

Since WSF/PHP is implemented in C, you can expect to have better performance while using it as compared to using a library written in PHP alone such as Zend Framework. However, the performance gain comes with a cost, that being the complexity of installing compiled C libraries as a PHP extension. Whereas a library written in PHP, such as Zend Framework, can be just copied to the document root and you are ready to use it.

Installing WSF/PHP

There is a comprehensive installation guide available online `http://wso2.org/project/wsf/php/2.0.0/docs/install_guide.html`. This guide explains Windows and Linux operating system specific steps that need to be followed in order to install the extension.

Implementing Services

There is a PHP class named WSService that comes with WSO2 WSF/PHP.

When you are implementing a service, you need to provide the set of operations and the set of REST semantics, including HTTP method and resource location.

Let's see how we can implement the book resource of the library system sample with WSO2 WSF/PHP.

```php
$service = new WSService(array (
    "operations" => $operations,
    "RESTMapping" => $restmap
));

$service->reply();
```

Operations and REST map are arrays provided to the service. The call to `reply()` method indicates that the service should go ahead and process the request.

Here is the operations array.

```php
$operations = array (
    "getBooks" => "getBooksFunction",
    "addBooks" => "addBooksFunction"
);
```

What we are doing here is that we map service operations to PHP functions that implement those operations. As an example, the `getBooks` operation would be handled by a function with the name `getBooksFunction`, defined in the PHP script. Note that these functions can take parameters, which we will see later in this chapter. However, when we define the options array, it is not required to mention the parameters of the functions. It is sufficient to mention only the name of the function irrespective of the type or number of parameters the functions would be accepting.

Here is the REST mapping array.

```php
$restmap = array (
    "getBooks" => array (
        "HTTPMethod" => "GET",
```

```
            "RESTLocation" => "book"
    ),
    "addBooks" => array (
        "HTTPMethod" => "POST",
        "RESTLocation" => "book"
    )
);
```

In here, we are providing the REST characteristics for the operations. As an example we specify that the getBooks operation would only respond to the GET requests and addBooks would respond to the POST requests. And both these operations are mapped to the location book. If the name of the PHP script with the service implementation is library.php and located in the folder /rest/09, the resource URL would be http://localhost/rest/09/library.php/book. As we saw in Chapter 4, while designing the sample Library service, a given business operation on a given resource does not get mapped to more than one HTTP verb. Hence in the operation mapping array more than one operation can be mapped to the same resource URL but with different HTTP verbs.

This design nicely maps to the resource design that we looked at while discussing the library system in Chapter 5.

URI	HTTP Method	Collection	Operation	Business Operation
/book	GET	books	retrieve	Get books
/book	POST	books	create	Add book(s)

In the implementation, we can cleanly map the resource location URI, the HTTP method required and the business operation.

Here is the getBooksFunction.

```
function getBooksFunction($inMessage) {
    $link = mysql_connect('localhost', 'sam', 'pass') or die('Could
not connect: ' . mysql_error());
    mysql_select_db('library') or die('Could not select database');

    $query = "SELECT b.id, b.name, b.author, b.isbn FROM book as b";

    $result = mysql_query($query) or die('Query failed: ' . mysql_
error());
    $response = "<books>";
    while ($line = mysql_fetch_array($result, MYSQL_ASSOC)) {
        $response .= "<book>";
        foreach ($line as $key => $col_value) {
            $response .= "<$key>$col_value</$key>";
```

```
        }
        $response .= "</book>";
    }
    $response .= "</books>";
    mysql_free_result($result);
    mysql_close($link);
    $outMessage = new WSMessage($response);
    return $outMessage;
}
```

In here, we are not interested in the input parameter as we are not expecting any. However, the operation function syntax mandates to have one, as the framework would fill in that if there were any input.

The response building logic should look familiar to you. We connect to the database, query for the book information and prepare the response XML string.

Finally, in this function, we create an instance of WSMessage with the response XML string that we prepared and returned.

```
        $outMessage = new WSMessage($response);
        return $outMessage;
```

If there is a return value, it is expected by the framework that you always return a WSMessage instance from the function implementing the operation business logic.

Next, the add book operation.

```
function addBooksFunction($inMessage) {
    $link = mysql_connect('localhost', 'sam', 'pass') or die('Could
not connect: ' . mysql_error());
    mysql_select_db('library') or die('Could not select database');
    $xml = simplexml_load_string($inMessage->str);
    foreach ($xml->book as $book) {
        $query = "INSERT INTO book (name, author, isbn) VALUES
('$book->name', '$book->author', '$book->isbn')";
        $result = mysql_query($query) or die('Query failed: ' . mysql_
error());
        mysql_free_result($result);
    }
    mysql_close($link);
    return;
}
```

In this operation, we pick the incoming XML request from the `in message`.

```
$xml = simplexml_load_string($inMessage->str);
```

Note that `$inMessage` is an instance of `WSMessage` class. `WSMessage` class captures the incoming XML request as a string and stores it in the `str` member variable.

And then `create new book` instances in the database which you are already familiar with.

Here is the complete PHP source code for the service.

```php
<?php
function getBooksFunction($inMessage) {
    $link = mysql_connect('localhost', 'sam', 'pass') or die('Could
not connect: ' . mysql_error());
    mysql_select_db('library') or die('Could not select database');
    $query = "SELECT b.id, b.name, b.author, b.isbn FROM book as b";
    $result = mysql_query($query) or die('Query failed: ' . mysql_
error());
    $response = "<books>";
    while ($line = mysql_fetch_array($result, MYSQL_ASSOC)) {
        $response .= "<book>";
        foreach ($line as $key => $col_value) {
            $response .= "<$key>$col_value</$key>";
        }
        $response .= "</book>";
    }
    $response .= "</books>";
    mysql_free_result($result);
    mysql_close($link);
    $outMessage = new WSMessage($response);
    return $outMessage;
}
function addBooksFunction($inMessage) {
    $link = mysql_connect('localhost', 'sam', 'pass') or die('Could
not connect: ' . mysql_error());
    mysql_select_db('library') or die('Could not select database');
    $xml = simplexml_load_string($inMessage->str);
    foreach ($xml->book as $book) {
        $query = "INSERT INTO book (name, author, isbn) VALUES
('$book->name', '$book->author', '$book->isbn')";
        $result = mysql_query($query) or die('Query failed: ' . mysql_
error());
```

```
            mysql_free_result($result);
        }
        mysql_close($link);

        return;
    }

    $operations = array (
        "getBooks" => "getBooksFunction",
        "addBooks" => "addBooksFunction"
    );

    $restmap = array (
        "getBooks" => array (
            "HTTPMethod" => "GET",
            "RESTLocation" => "book"
        ),
        "addBooks" => array (
            "HTTPMethod" => "POST",
            "RESTLocation" => "book"
        )
    );

    $service = new WSService(array (
        "operations" => $operations,
        "RESTMapping" => $restmap
    ));

    $service->reply();
?>
```

Implementing Clients

Implementing clients with WSF/PHP is very simple. Here is the code to list
the books.

```
<?php
$requestPayloadString = <<<XML
<getBooks>
        <book/>
</getBooks>
XML;

try {

    $client = new WSClient( array("to" => "http://localhost/rest/09/
library.php/book",

                                  "useSOAP" => FALSE,
```

```
                              "HTTPMethod" => "GET"));
    $responseMessage = $client->request($requestPayloadString);
    printf("Response = %s <br>", htmlspecialchars($responseMessage-
>str));
} catch (Exception $e) {
    if ($e instanceof WSFault) {
        printf("Error String: %s\n", $e->str);
        printf("HTTP Code    : %s\n", $e->httpStatusCode);
    } else {
        printf("Message = %s\n",$e->getMessage());
    }
}
?>
```

There is a PHP class named WSClient that comes with WSO2 WSF/PHP. While creating the client object instance you can provide an array of options. The options could include the endpoint address of the service, the "to" option. To make use of REST you have to set the "useSOAP" to FALSE. You can also specify the HTTP method to be used with "HTTPMethod" option.

```
    $client = new WSClient( array("to" => "http://localhost/rest/09/
library.php/book",
                            "useSOAP" => FALSE,
                            "HTTPMethod" => "GET"));
```

Then you send the request and receive the response.

```
    $responseMessage = $client->request($requestPayloadString);
```

In this sample the request payload could be empty but in case you want to send a set of query parameters, you can provide that as XML and the framework would encode that into a series of query parameters.

Finally, you can consume the response.

```
    printf("Response = %s <br>", htmlspecialchars($responseMessage->str));
```

If there are any errors, you can use the exception model to deal with them with WSO2 WSF/PHP. In this sample, we have a try catch block.

```
    } catch (Exception $e) {
        if ($e instanceof WSFault) {
            printf("Error String: %s\n", $e->str);
            printf("HTTP Code    : %s\n", $e->httpStatusCode);
        } else {
            printf("Message = %s\n",$e->getMessage());
        }
    }
}
```

In case of errors, the framework would compose the error message to a WSFault instance.

Next we will see the client code that adds books.

```php
<?php
$requestPayloadString = <<<XML
<books>
    <book><name>Book7</name><author>Auth7</author><isbn>ISBN0007</isbn></book>
    <book><name>Book8</name><author>Auth8</author><isbn>ISBN0008</isbn></book>
</books>
XML;
try {
    $client = new WSClient( array("to" => "http://localhost/rest/09/library.php/book",
                                  "useSOAP" => FALSE,
                                  "HTTPMethod" => "POST"));
    $client->request($requestPayloadString);
} catch (Exception $e) {
    if ($e instanceof WSFault) {
        printf("Error String: %s\n", $e->str);
        printf("HTTP Code    : %s\n", $e->httpStatusCode);
    } else {
        printf("Message = %s\n",$e->getMessage());
    }
}
?>
```

The only differences in this client code and the previous GET client is the fact that we use a different XML request payload expected by the add operation. We use HTTP POST method instead of GET and the fact that we are not expecting a response from the server.

SOAP Service and Client

As mentioned earlier, one of the advantages of WSF/PHP framework is the ability to use a given service both as a REST style service as well as a SOAP style service.

The good news is that you do not need to change any code in the service script to make it a SOAP service. You can use the same service that we implemented under the service implementation section above and send a SOAP request to the service and receive a SOAP response from the service. It is a feature of WSF/PHP framework for services to respond to clients based on the request format the clients use.

In order to write a SOAP client for the same service we can use the same client code that we used in the above section for implementing REST client and do a few minor modifications.

The first modification is to change the URL slightly. In the REST client, while creating WSClient, we used the following "to" option.

```
"to" => "http://localhost/rest/09/library.php/book"
```

For the SOAP client, we have to modify this to

```
"to" => "http://localhost/rest/09/library.php"
```

Note that we have removed the trailing /book section from the URL. This is because, while using SOAP, unlike in the case of REST, we do not use the concept of a resource. We just have to use the name of the root service, in this case, library.php.

The next change is to instruct the client to use the SOAP message format. In the REST client, we used the option:

```
"useSOAP" => FALSE
```

For the SOAP client, we could use the option:

```
"useSOAP" => TRUE
```

We could also remove this option for the SOAP client because if this option is not present, WSClient class assumes the SOAP message format by default.

The third and final change required to convert the REST client to a SOAP client with the WSF/PHP is to remove the HTTP method option. In the REST client we used:

```
"HTTPMethod" => "GET"
```

In case of SOAP clients and services the usual HTTP method used is POST. In other words, while using SOAP, the HTTP verb being used is not significant. This is one of the key differences between the SOAP style services and REST style services.

Here is the complete source code for the SOAP client with WSF/PHP for the library service.

```php
<?php
$requestPayloadString = <<<XML
<getBooks>
        <book/>
</getBooks>
XML;

try {
```

```php
        $client = new WSClient( array("to" => "http://localhost/rest/09/
library.php",

                                  "useSOAP" => TRUE));

        $responseMessage = $client->request($requestPayloadString);

        printf("Response = %s <br>", htmlspecialchars($responseMessage-
>str));

} catch (Exception $e) {
    if ($e instanceof WSFault) {
        printf("Error String: %s\n", $e->str);
        printf("HTTP Code   : %s\n", $e->httpStatusCode);
    } else {
        printf("Message = %s\n",$e->getMessage());
    }
}
?>
```

If you use the SOAP client in place of the REST client, you would not see much behaviour difference in the client, in other words, both REST and SOAP clients would give you the same output. However, if you capture the messages that go over the wire while using the SOAP and REST clients and compare them, you will notice a drastic difference in the message formats.

Here is the REST request sent by the REST client.

```
GET /rest/09/library.php/book HTTP/1.1
User-Agent: Axis2C/1.5.0
Host: localhost
```

Here is the SOAP request sent by the SOAP client.

```
POST /rest/09/library.php HTTP/1.1
User-Agent: Axis2C/1.5.0
Content-Length: 177
Content-Type: application/soap+xml;charset=UTF-8
Host: localhost

<soapenv:Envelope xmlns:soapenv="http://www.w3.org/2003/05/
soap-envelope">
    <soapenv:Header/>
    <soapenv:Body>
        <getBooks>
            <book/>
        </getBooks>
    </soapenv:Body></soapenv:Envelope>
```

As you would immediately notice, the SOAP request is much more bulky than the REST request. This is one of the key criticisms that SOAP gets, and one of the key reasons why people prefer REST over SOAP.

You could notice the same in the responses as well. The response to REST client from the service would look like the following.

```
HTTP/1.1 200 OK
Date: Sun, 28 Sep 2008 02:58:25 GMT
Server: Apache/2.2.6 (Win32) mod_ssl/2.2.6 OpenSSL/0.9.8e PHP/5.2.5
X-Powered-By: PHP/5.2.5
Content-Length: 314
Content-Type: text/xml;charset=UTF-8

<books>
    <book>
        <id>1</id>
        <name>Book1</name>
        <author>Auth1</author>
        <isbn>ISBN0001</isbn>
    </book>
    <book>
        <id>2</id>
        <name>Book2</name>
        <author>Auth2</author>
        <isbn>ISBN0002</isbn>
    </book>
    <book>
        <id>3</id>
        <name>Book3</name>
        <author>Auth3</author>
        <isbn>ISBN0003</isbn>
    </book>
    <book>
        <id>29</id>
        <name/>
        <author/>
        <isbn/>
    </book>
</books>
```

The response from the service to the SOAP client would be:

```
HTTP/1.1 200 OK
Date: Sun, 28 Sep 2008 02:59:27 GMT
Server: Apache/2.2.6 (Win32) mod_ssl/2.2.6 OpenSSL/0.9.8e PHP/5.2.5
```

```
X-Powered-By: PHP/5.2.5
Content-Length: 453
Content-Type: application/soap+xml;charset=UTF-8

<soapenv:Envelope xmlns:soapenv="http://www.w3.org/2003/05/soap-
envelope">
    <soapenv:Header/>
    <soapenv:Body>
        <books>
            <book>
                <id>1</id>
                <name>Book1</name>
                <author>Auth1</author>
                <isbn>ISBN0001</isbn>
            </book>
            <book>
                <id>2</id>
                <name>Book2</name>
                <author>Auth2</author>
                <isbn>ISBN0002</isbn>
            </book>
            <book>
                <id>3</id>
                <name>Book3</name>
                <author>Auth3</author>
                <isbn>ISBN0003</isbn>
            </book>
            <book>
                <id>29</id>
                <name/>
                <author/>
                <isbn/>
            </book>
        </books>
    </soapenv:Body>
</soapenv:Envelope>
```

The difference between SOAP and REST response messages are not as drastic as the request messages, but still, note the wrapping elements that SOAP uses in the response compared to the REST response, that makes even the response message slightly larger.

When the number of interactions increase, the additional overhead in the SOAP messaging style would account considerable overhead. Hence REST style would be the preferred style.

However, there are situations where SOAP is being used in the industry, especially in the enterprise. If you want to sign and encrypt the messages to secure the interactions, and if you want to make the same secure interaction reliable, SOAP has provision for them and the bulky message format comes into use.

Summary

WSO2 WSF/PHP framework, `http://wso2.org/projects/wsf/php`, provides comprehensive support for implementing REST style services and clients. The framework provides an API that makes it easy to map design to the implementation.

In this chapter, we discussed how to use WSF/PHP service and client API to implement the sample library system as a REST service, and implemented a REST client to consume the same. We also looked into using the SOAP features provided in the frameworks to implement a SOAP client to consume the same service using SOAP style messages.

We also discussed the differences between REST and SOAP message styles.

You can try the samples that are available online at `http://labs.wso2.org/wsf/php/`.

B
RESTClient class

Here is a simple `RESTClient` class that you can use to consume services.

The name of the PHP class is `RESTClient`. This class does not use any other framework and is based solely on basic PHP constructs. Hence you can easily use this class on its own without having to install any other framework. This would be useful if you want to just consume services using some lightweight PHP code.

We use a private variable in the PHP code to track whether to use CURL or not based on the availability of CURL in the PHP system installed.

```php
private $with_curl;
```

While creating an instance of the client, the constructor of the class either chooses to use CURL if the CURL functions are available or else it would use `fopen` functions for communicating with the services.

```php
public function __construct() {
    if (function_exists("curl_init")) {
        $this->with_curl = TRUE;
    } else {
        $this->with_curl = FALSE;
    }
}
```

The `RESTClient` class has four member functions `get`, `post`, `put`, and `delete` to work with HTTP verbs GET, POST, PUT and DELETE respectively. While using these methods of the class we must pay attention to the parameters that each method takes.

get Method

The get member function of RESTClient class takes two parameters, the URL of the service and the request parameters.

```php
public function get($url, $params) {
```

And it builds the request URL to include the request parameters.

```php
$params_str = "?";
if (is_array($params)) {
    foreach ($params as $key => $value) {
        $params_str .= urlencode($key) . "=" .
urlencode($value) . "&";
    }
} else {
    $params_str .= $params;
}

$url .= $params_str;
```

And if CURL is available, it would send a GET request using CURL.

```php
if ($this->with_curl) {
    $curl = curl_init();
    curl_setopt($curl, CURLOPT_URL, $url);
    curl_setopt($curl, CURLOPT_HTTPGET, TRUE);
    curl_setopt($curl, CURLOPT_USERAGENT, RESTClient ::
                                        USER_AGENT);
    $result = curl_exec($curl);
    curl_close($curl);
}
```

We are already familiar with the constructs used in the above method that were discussed in Chapter 2.

If CURL is not available, we would be using fopen function to send the GET request and fetch the result.

```php
} else {
    $opts = array (
        'http' => array (
            'method' => "GET",
            'header' => "User-Agent: " . RESTClient ::
                        USER_AGENT . "\r\n"
        )
    );
```

```
        $context = stream_context_create($opts);

        $fp = fopen($url, 'r', false, $context);
        $result = fpassthru($fp);
        fclose($fp);
    }
```

In here, we use the options to be used with the HTTP request such as the HTTP method GET and user agent header. We then create a context with those options and open the URL with fopen, using the context created.

post Method

The post method takes three parameters, the service URL, data to be posted and an optional third parameter that specifies the content type.

```
    public function post($url, $data, $content_type = "application
/x-www-form-urlencoded") {
```

If CURL is available, the given data would be posted to the given service URL.

```
        if ($this->with_curl) {
            $curl = curl_init();
            curl_setopt($curl, CURLOPT_HTTPHEADER, Array (
                "Content-Type: " . $content_type
            ));
            curl_setopt($curl, CURLOPT_URL, $url);
            curl_setopt($curl, CURLOPT_POST, TRUE);
            curl_setopt($curl, CURLOPT_POSTFIELDS, $data);
            curl_setopt($curl, CURLOPT_RETURNTRANSFER, true);
            curl_setopt($curl, CURLOPT_USERAGENT, RESTClient ::
            USER_AGENT);
            $result = curl_exec($curl);
            curl_close($curl);
        }
```

We set the content type as an HTTP header. So if the user of the class provided a custom content type that would be reflected in the request sent to the service. Again, the CURL POST syntax used in this method was discussed in Chapter 2 in detail.

If CURL is not available, as in the case of get method, we use fopen to get the job done.

```
        } else {
            $opts = array (
                'http' => array (
                    'method' => "POST",
```

```
        'header' => "User-Agent: " . RESTClient ::
                        USER_AGENT . "\r\n" .
            "Content-Type: " . $content_type . "\r\n" .
            "Content-length: " . strlen($data
        ) . "\r\n",
        'content' => $data
));

$context = stream_context_create($opts);

$fp = fopen($url, 'r', false, $context);
$result = fpassthru($fp);
fclose($fp);
}
```

put Method

The put method takes two parameters, the service URL and data to be put to
the service.

```
public function put($url, $data) {
```

While using PUT with CURL, we need to have a file handler with the data to be sent
to service with PUT. So we create a file handler in memory first and then write the
data given by the user to that file handler.

```
$fh = fopen('php://memory', 'rw');
fwrite($fh, $data);
rewind($fh);
```

Then we put that data to the service using CURL.

```
$curl = curl_init();

curl_setopt($curl, CURLOPT_USERAGENT, RESTClient ::
                                        USER_AGENT);
curl_setopt($curl, CURLOPT_INFILE, $fh);
curl_setopt($curl, CURLOPT_INFILESIZE, strlen($data));
curl_setopt($curl, CURLOPT_TIMEOUT, 10);
curl_setopt($curl, CURLOPT_PUT, 1);
curl_setopt($curl, CURLOPT_URL, $url);
curl_setopt($curl, CURLOPT_RETURNTRANSFER, true);
$result = curl_exec($curl);
curl_close($curl);

fclose($fh);
```

If CURL is not present, we again use `fopen` to handle the PUT request.

```php
    } else {
        $opts = array (
            'http' => array (
                'method' => "PUT",
                'header' => "User-Agent: " . RESTClient ::
                                USER_AGENT . "\r\n" .
                "Content-Type: " . $content_type . "\r\n" .
                "Content-length: " . strlen($data
            ) . "\r\n",
                'content' => $data
        ));
        $context = stream_context_create($opts);
        $fp = fopen($url, 'r', false, $context);
        $result = fpassthru($fp);
        fclose($fp);
    }
```

delete Method

The `delete` method takes two parameters, the service URL and request parameters to be used with delete request to the service.

As in the case of GET requests, we use the request parameters and build the URL with the request parameters in place.

```php
        $params_str = "?";
        if (is_array($params)) {
            foreach ($params as $key => $value) {
                $params_str .= urlencode($key) . "=" .
urlencode($value) . "&";
            }
        } else {
            $params_str .= $params;
        }
        $url .= $params_str;
```

Then if CURL is present, we send the DELETE request to the service URL with CURL.

```php
        if ($this->with_curl) {
            $curl = curl_init();
            curl_setopt($curl, CURLOPT_URL, $url);
            curl_setopt($curl, CURLOPT_CUSTOMREQUEST, "delete");
```

```
            curl_setopt($curl, CURLOPT_USERAGENT, RESTClient ::
                                                  USER_AGENT);

            $result = curl_exec($curl);
            curl_close($curl);
        }
```

If CURL is not present, we use the `fopen` logic.

```
        } else {
            $opts = array (
                'http' => array (
                    'method' => "DELETE",
                    'header' => "User-Agent: " . RESTClient ::
                                USER_AGENT . "\r\n"
                )
            );

            $context = stream_context_create($opts);

            $fp = fopen($url, 'r', false, $context);
            $result = fpassthru($fp);
            fclose($fp);

        }
```

Complete RESTClient Class

```php
<?php
class RESTClient {
    private $with_curl;

    const USER_AGENT = 'RESTClient';

    /*
     * Constructor of the RESTClient
     */
    public function __construct() {
        if (function_exists("curl_init")) {
            $this->with_curl = TRUE;
        } else {
            $this->with_curl = FALSE;
        }
    }
    /*
     * Call the HTTP 'GET' method
     * @param string $url URL of the service.
     * @param array $params request parameters, hash of
                                            (key,value) pairs
```

```php
     * @return response string
     */
    public function get($url, $params) {
        $params_str = "?";
        if (is_array($params)) {
            foreach ($params as $key => $value) {
                $params_str .= urlencode($key) . "=" .
urlencode($value) . "&";
            }
        } else {
            $params_str .= $params;
        }

        $url .= $params_str;

        $result = "";

        if ($this->with_curl) {
            $curl = curl_init();
            curl_setopt($curl, CURLOPT_URL, $url);
            curl_setopt($curl, CURLOPT_HTTPGET, TRUE);
            curl_setopt($curl, CURLOPT_USERAGENT, RESTClient ::
                                                USER_AGENT);
            curl_setopt($curl, CURLOPT_RETURNTRANSFER, TRUE);
            $result = curl_exec($curl);
            curl_close($curl);
        } else {
            $opts = array (
                'http' => array (
                    'method' => "GET",
                    'header' => "User-Agent: " . RESTClient ::
                                                USER_AGENT . "\r\n"
                )
            );

            $context = stream_context_create($opts);

            $fp = fopen($url, 'r', false, $context);
            $result = fpassthru($fp);
            fclose($fp);
        }

        return $result;
    }

    /*
     * Call the HTTP 'POST' method
     * @param string $url URL of the service..
     * @param string $data request data
```

```php
 * @param array $content_type the http content type
 * @return response string
 */
public function post($url, $data, $content_type = "application
                                 /x-www-form-urlencoded") {
    $result = "";
    if ($this->with_curl) {
        $curl = curl_init();
        curl_setopt($curl, CURLOPT_HTTPHEADER, Array (
            "Content-Type: " . $content_type
        ));
        curl_setopt($curl, CURLOPT_URL, $url);
        curl_setopt($curl, CURLOPT_POST, TRUE);
        curl_setopt($curl, CURLOPT_POSTFIELDS, $data);
        curl_setopt($curl, CURLOPT_RETURNTRANSFER, true);
        curl_setopt($curl, CURLOPT_USERAGENT, RESTClient ::
                                         USER_AGENT);
        $result = curl_exec($curl);
        curl_close($curl);
    } else {
        $opts = array (
            'http' => array (
                'method' => "POST",
                'header' => "User-Agent: " . RESTClient ::
                            USER_AGENT . "\r\n" .
                "Content-Type: " . $content_type . "\r\n" .
                "Content-length: " . strlen($data
            ) . "\r\n",
                'content' => $data
        ));
        $context = stream_context_create($opts);
        $fp = fopen($url, 'r', false, $context);
        $result = fpassthru($fp);
        fclose($fp);
    }
    return $result;
}
/*
 * Call the HTTP 'PUT' method
 * @param string $url URL of the service..
 * @param string $data request data
 * @return response string
 */
```

```php
public function put($url, $data) {
    $result = "";

    if ($this->with_curl) {
        $fh = fopen('php://memory', 'rw');
        fwrite($fh, $data);
        rewind($fh);

        $curl = curl_init();
        curl_setopt($curl, CURLOPT_USERAGENT, RESTClient ::
                                                    USER_AGENT);
        curl_setopt($curl, CURLOPT_INFILE, $fh);
        curl_setopt($curl, CURLOPT_INFILESIZE, strlen($data));
        curl_setopt($curl, CURLOPT_TIMEOUT, 10);
        curl_setopt($curl, CURLOPT_PUT, 1);
        curl_setopt($curl, CURLOPT_URL, $url);
        curl_setopt($curl, CURLOPT_RETURNTRANSFER, true);
        $result = curl_exec($curl);
        curl_close($curl);

        fclose($fh);

    } else {
        $opts = array (
            'http' => array (
                'method' => "PUT",
                'header' => "User-Agent: " . RESTClient ::
                                            USER_AGENT . "\r\n" .
                "Content-Type: " . $content_type . "\r\n" .
                "Content-length: " . strlen($data
            ) . "\r\n",
            'content' => $data
        ));

        $context = stream_context_create($opts);

        $fp = fopen($url, 'r', false, $context);
        $result = fpassthru($fp);
        fclose($fp);
    }

    return $result;
}
/*
 * Call the HTTP 'DELETE' method
 * @param string $url URL of the service..
 * @param array $params request parameters, hash of
                                            (key,value) pairs

 */
```

```php
        public function delete($url, $params) {
            $params_str = "?";
            if (is_array($params)) {
                foreach ($params as $key => $value) {
                    $params_str .= urlencode($key) . "=" .
urlencode($value) . "&";
                }
            } else {
                $params_str .= $params;
            }

            $url .= $params_str;

            $result = "";

            if ($this->with_curl) {
                $curl = curl_init();
                curl_setopt($curl, CURLOPT_URL, $url);
                curl_setopt($curl, CURLOPT_CUSTOMREQUEST, "delete");
                curl_setopt($curl, CURLOPT_USERAGENT, RESTClient ::
                                                    USER_AGENT);

                $result = curl_exec($curl);
                curl_close($curl);
            } else {
                $opts = array (
                    'http' => array (
                        'method' => "DELETE",
                        'header' => "User-Agent: " . RESTClient ::
                                                    USER_AGENT . "\r\n"
                    )
                );

                $context = stream_context_create($opts);

                $fp = fopen($url, 'r', false, $context);
                $result = fpassthru($fp);
                fclose($fp);
            }
        }
    }
?>
```

get Example

Let's use the RESTClient class to consume some services. Let us use the library example service from previous chapters first. Here is the PHP client code for getting the books.

```php
<?php
require "RESTClient.php";

$client = new RESTClient();
$result = $client->get(
    "http://localhost/rest/09/library.php/book", array());

printf("Response = %s <br>", htmlspecialchars($result));
?>
```

First, we indicate that we require the source file with RESTClient PHP class. We use a require statement to do this. Obviously, we assume that the PHP class is defined in a file with the name RESTClient.php.

```php
require "RESTClient.php";
```

Next we create an instance of the RESTClient class.

```php
$client = new RESTClient();
```

And we send a GET request to the service URL.

```php
$result = $client->get(
    "http://localhost/rest/09/library.php/book", array());
```

Note that the request parameters array is empty because we do not have any parameters to be sent to the service.

Finally we print out the result.

```php
printf("Response = %s <br>", htmlspecialchars($result));
```

Note how the use of the RESTClient class has simplified our PHP code to consume the service a great deal.

post Example

Let's also look at how to use RESTClient class for a POST request with the
library service.

```php
<?php
require "RESTClient.php";

$data = <<<XML
<books>
    <book><name>Book7</name><author>Auth7</author><isbn>ISBN0007</isbn></book>
    <book><name>Book8</name><author>Auth8</author><isbn>ISBN0008</isbn></book>
</books>
XML;

$client = new RESTClient();
$client->post("http://localhost/rest/09/library.php/book", $data,
"text/xml");
?>
```

As in the case of the sample used to GET data, the POST sample is very simple. First
require the PHP file with the class implementation.

```php
require "RESTClient.php";
```

Then we define the data that we want to be posted to the service.

```php
$data = <<<XML
<books>
    <book><name>Book7</name><author>Auth7</author><isbn>ISBN0007</isbn></book>
    <book><name>Book8</name><author>Auth8</author><isbn>ISBN0008</isbn></book>
</books>
XML;
```

Next, create the RESTClient class instance.

```php
$client = new RESTClient();
```

And post the data to the service.

```php
$client->post("http://localhost/rest/09/library.php/book", $data,
"text/xml");
```

Note that we have used the third parameter with the value text/xml to indicate that
we are posting XML data to the service.

Yahoo Search Client Example

Let's see how to use `RESTClient` class to consume the Yahoo spelling suggestion service.

```php
<?php
require "RESTClient.php";

$client = new RESTClient();
$result = $client->get(
            "http://search.yahooapis.com/WebSearchService/V1/
                spellingSuggestion",
            array( "appid" => "YahooDemo",
                    "query" => "apocalipto"));
printf("Response = %s <br>", htmlspecialchars($result));
?>
```

First we require the PHP file with the class implementation.

```php
require "RESTClient.php";
```

Next, create the `RESTClient` class instance.

```php
$client = new RESTClient();
```

And send the GET request to the service.

```php
$result = $client->get(
            "http://search.yahooapis.com/WebSearchService/V1/
                spellingSuggestion",
            array( "appid" => "YahooDemo",
                    "query" => "apocalipto"));
```

Note that in addition to the service location URL, used as the first parameter, we have used the service request parameters as an array in the second parameter.

Summary

In this chapter, we introduced a PHP class named `RESTClient` that can be used to consume REST style services. This class supports all key HTTP verbs, GET, POST, PUT and DELETE.

The advantage of using such a class is that it minimizes the complexity of your client code. At the same time you can re-use this class for all your REST style client implementations. This PHP class is sufficient for most simple REST style client programs and requires no third-party libraries. However, if you want to implement services and also want advanced clients, it is advised that you use more established framework such as Zend Framework or WSO2 WSF/PHP.

Index

Y

Yahoo news search, REST services
  logical script breakdown 59, 60
  news, displaying 60
  URL 60
Yahoo search client example 197

Z

Zend_Rest_Client
  using 128
Zend_Rest_Server
  using 126
  using, example 126, 127

Zend framework
  about 125
  features 125
  installing 125
Zend Framework, PHP REST
      frameworks 20
Zend REST classes
  library system, implementing 129
Zend REST classes library system
  library clients 141
  library services 129
  library services, implementing 130

Thank you for buying
RESTful PHP Web Services

Packt Open Source Project Royalties

When we sell a book written on an Open Source project, we pay a royalty directly to that project. Therefore by purchasing RESTful PHP Web Services, Packt will have given some of the money received to the PHP project.

In the long term, we see ourselves and you — customers and readers of our books — as part of the Open Source ecosystem, providing sustainable revenue for the projects we publish on. Our aim at Packt is to establish publishing royalties as an essential part of the service and support a business model that sustains Open Source.

If you're working with an Open Source project that you would like us to publish on, and subsequently pay royalties to, please get in touch with us.

Writing for Packt

We welcome all inquiries from people who are interested in authoring. Book proposals should be sent to author@packtpub.com. If your book idea is still at an early stage and you would like to discuss it first before writing a formal book proposal, contact us; one of our commissioning editors will get in touch with you.

We're not just looking for published authors; if you have strong technical skills but no writing experience, our experienced editors can help you develop a writing career, or simply get some additional reward for your expertise.

About Packt Publishing

Packt, pronounced 'packed', published its first book "Mastering phpMyAdmin for Effective MySQL Management" in April 2004 and subsequently continued to specialize in publishing highly focused books on specific technologies and solutions.

Our books and publications share the experiences of your fellow IT professionals in adapting and customizing today's systems, applications, and frameworks. Our solution-based books give you the knowledge and power to customize the software and technologies you're using to get the job done. Packt books are more specific and less general than the IT books you have seen in the past. Our unique business model allows us to bring you more focused information, giving you more of what you need to know, and less of what you don't.

Packt is a modern, yet unique publishing company, which focuses on producing quality, cutting-edge books for communities of developers, administrators, and newbies alike. For more information, please visit our website: www.PacktPub.com.

Object-Oriented Programming with PHP5

ISBN: 978-1-847192-56-1   Paperback: 250 pages

Learn to leverage PHP5's OOP features to write manageable applications with ease

1. General OOP concepts explained

2. Implement Design Patterns in your applications and solve common OOP Problems

3. Take full advantage of native built-in objects

4. Test your code by writing unit tests with PHPUnit

PHP Web 2.0 Mashup Projects

ISBN: 978-1-847190-88-8   Paperback: 280 pages

Create practical mashups in PHP grabbing and mixing data from Google Maps, Flickr, Amazon, YouTube, MSN Search, Yahoo!, Last.fm, and 411Sync.com

1. Expand your website and applications using mashups

2. Gain a thorough understanding of mashup fundamentals

3. Clear, detailed walk-through of the key PHP mashup building technologies

4. Five fully implemented example mashups with full code

Please check **www.PacktPub.com** for information on our titles

PHP Oracle Web Development

ISBN: 978-1-847193-63-6   Paperback: 350 pages

A practical guide to combining the power, performance, scalability, and reliability of the Oracle Database with the ease of use, short development time, and high performance of PHP

1. Program your own PHP/Oracle application

2. Move data processing inside the database

3. Distribute data processing between the web/PHP and Oracle database servers

4. Create reusable building blocks for PHP/Oracle solutions

PHP 5 CMS Framework Development

ISBN: 978-1-847193-57-5   Paperback: 328 pages

Expert insight and practical guidance to creating an efficient, flexible, and robust framework for a PHP 5-based content management system

1. Learn how to design, build, and implement a complete CMS framework for your custom requirements

2. Implement a solid architecture with object orientation, MVC

3. Build an infrastructure for custom menus, modules, components, sessions, user tracking, and more

4. Written by a seasoned developer of CMS applications

Please check **www.PacktPub.com** for information on our titles

5023216R0

Made in the USA
Lexington, KY
26 March 2010